Sabre Competition & Scouting Journal

Fencing Journal Series

Lisa Campi-Sapery

Sabre Competition & Scouting Journal
Fencing Journal Series

Copyright © 2018 Lisa Campi-Sapery
Cover art by Lisa Campi-Sapery

thefencingref.com

All rights reserved. No part of this book may be reproduced in any manner without written permission except in the case of brief quotations included in critical articles and reviews. For information, please contact the author.

First Edition

ISBN: 171707491X
ISBN-13: 978-1717074911

ACKNOWLEDGEMENTS

There are so many people I am grateful for in this long journey in fencing.

First, fencing gave me my ability to be a complete and total bad ass. So let your fencing journey be one of empowerment.

I am grateful to the teams and teammates that supported and shaped me:
Morris Hills High School
Salle Santelli New Jersey
University of North Carolina at Chapel Hill
Fencing Academy of Philadelphia
and the last club I will ever represent – Forte Fencing.

Second, it gave me family of all kinds. My parents were so profoundly supportive of my fencing. My sister, the amazing Barb Lynch, got me started, and she got her kids hooked on the sport too: my Patrick and Fiona. And then there are the loved ones that the sport has given me: Coach, Jelena, Alex, Melissa, Ivona, Monica, Alice, Adam, Willamina, Cheryl, George, Steve, Keri, Jackson, Mike, Tony, Rob, and countless others who I will realize I forgot the minute this is published.

Then there are the children given to me by the universe:
Andrew "Lefty," Jaime, Zack, Ryan, David, Jackson, Hudson
and my two sons who left us far too soon, Phil and Matt.

Lastly, I must express my gratitude to my husband. I was so lucky that, after 25 years of friendship, he was brave enough to ask me out. I had no idea anything was missing until he came into my life. Somehow an independent, fearless, and fierce woman found her soulmate and can't imagine life without him.

Lisa

CONTENTS

About this book 1

Information About Me 5

Tournament Schedule/Results 6

Timeline for Tournament Planning 8

Packing Checklist 9

Fencing Hydration and Nutrition 10

Scoresheets and Tournament Evaluation (example) 12

Pool Bout Orders 18

Scoresheets and Tournament Evaluation 20

Scouting (example) 170

Scouting (practice) 171

Scouting Journal 175

ABOUT THIS BOOK
(read this – seriously – read this, it will help you.)

"Never memorize something that you can look up."
~Albert Einstein

When I first went to find a tournament journal/scouting book for my fencing students, I thought, "Surely there must be something already out there." What I found were cute books with blank pages but little organization. The tournament pages were incomplete and disjointed. Furthermore, there was no place for an athlete to keep records and to scout their opponents. And I thought the journals would be improved if they were weapon-specific.

When an athlete is trying to become a better fencer, a blank book only helps if that person knows what to write. I was told by my coach to take a notebook with me to every fencing tournament and to write down information about the opponents in my pool. I began to realize that I was creating reference material; information I would want to refer back to the next time I fenced that person.

The main thing I learned was that one of the best ways to become a better fencer is to document your tournament, plan for the next event, and have scouting information about opponents to use for the next time you face them.

Picture a new fencer. She has scouted her opponent and knows that she is good at circular parries. But this new fencer has trouble with feints and finishes around a defense like that (as do many new fencers). Prior to the bout, she practices some advance-lunges with a feint-deceive, in hopes that if there is an opportunity to use that, she will be able to execute it freely.

Be careful what you do with this information, though. Some athletes will over-process and, for them, "paralysis by analysis" is a genuine concern. Some fencing athletes tighten up in a bout because they are too worried about all the "what if's" that could occur. This is yet another advantage to scouting, because it will help you create a game plan prior to the bout. In essence, having a plan can lessen the anxiety and stress of fencing. Always remember that the actual bout is a fluid thing, and sometimes a plan of action needs to be modified, changed, or sometimes even abandoned. Talk to your coach about how to handle each of these situations.

So how will this journal help me? Instead of just pool sheets and direct elimination pages, this book is designed to help you organize, evaluate, and scout during your day of competition. You will be able to: document a tournament, do some quick scouting during your pool, detail more-formal scouting for future use, and evaluate your performance as a whole. Writing down what happened is fine, however the best athletes and coaches will "debrief" after events. This journal uses the "Coach Lisa 10-10-10" system of debriefing: ten things you need to work on, ten solutions to those things, and ten things you did well.

Each section has a sample page (or row) to help you get started. It may seem daunting at first, but each time you write an entry, you will become more comfortable with it. You will eventually find yourself using this journal's guidance more and more to improve your skill in competition.

The final and largest section of this journal is comprised of the scouting pages; sort of an "address book" where you will document: who you fenced, when you fenced, the outcome, and what worked or didn't work. Many years ago, I used an old-school "little black book" to conduct this scouting. You don't have to – it's all here.

Just like fencing, the best way to get acquainted with using this journal is practice. Only in the introduction, and you already have homework? Yes, but this is fun homework. Go online and watch a fencing video in your weapon. It can be of any level, but I think the higher the level, the better. There are blank scouting pages included starting on page 171 so you can practice your scouting. I found it fun to scout Zagunis, Kharlan, or Montano. This practice will help get you used to identifying the critical aspects of their game and how to use the scouting form's layout in ways that resonate with your brain.

How do I recommend you use this book?

1. Read through all of the samples and tips, and fill out the practice pages. Most importantly, do NOT get overwhelmed. There are tips for competition, tips for hydration, and tips for competition eating. There is even a timeline leading up to a tournament, outlining when you should be testing your weapons and cords, packing your gear and foodstuffs, and preparing yourself. Lastly, there is a checklist so you don't forget to pack anything vital.

2. Buy small Post-it Notes or paper clips (I recommend the multi-colored ones). On competition day, use them to make tabs:

    - One that says "BOUT ORDER" on page 18.
    - One saying "TODAY" on the next blank Pool Sheet (first one starts on page 20)
    - One per opponent in the alphabetical Scouting section (last names beginning with "A" start on page 175). After the pool (or even during) you can write detailed information about each opponent.

    Note: Parents/spouses/friends can help with this, if you wish (and it works best if they have some fencing knowledge). That is why the DE sheets have space for each touch – so support people can help. However, when it comes to scouting, remember that everyone's brain works differently, and you're the one who needs to fully understand what's being noted.

3. Don't put away that scouting book after you are eliminated. Scouting and observing fencers after you are knocked out (especially the one who beat you) will help you get better.

4. It is best to evaluate your whole tournament as soon as feasible, while your memory is still fresh. If you are still upset about losing your last DE, hold off entering anything. I recommend giving yourself 15 minutes to wallow. Set a timer, stew, don't throw anything valuable (find a quiet, solitary place to throw something like a beanbag against a wall – don't harm yourself, your fencing gear, nor the facility). But don't leave post-tournament evaluation for too much later when you might have forgotten details. Fair warning: the Ten Things You Did Well are the toughest part of the tournament evaluation. While it is easy to be self-critical, it is more difficult to be self-praising. With time, the whole process of evaluation gets easier.

5. Next competition, use your scouting. The next time you fence that person, you will have vital reference information and be able to fence your best!

Now you are ready to start. Read through this book to get yourself familiar with it. Good luck, and know that this journal-scouting book will help you become a better competitive fencer.

> *"A journey of a thousand miles begins with just one step."*
> ~Lao Tzu

INFORMATION ABOUT ME

Name:
Phone:
Email:

Started Fencing:
Club(s):
Coach(es):

Season:

Sabre Classifications:

	Earned	Re-earned	Re-earned	Re-earned
E				
D				
C				
B				
A				

TOURNAMENT SCHEDULE/RESULTS

Tournament	Age Group or Category	Event Date	Deadline to Register	Date Registered	Total Entries	My Final Place	Points or Classification Earned	Post Competition Evaluation?
Cobra SYC	Y-14	11/25/17	10/24/17	10/16/17	48	12th	83.2	✓

Tournament	Age Group or Category	Event Date	Deadline to Register	Date Registered	Total Entries	My Final Place	Points or Classification Earned	Post Competition Evaluation?

TIMELINE FOR TOURNAMENT PLANNING

Planning for a major tournament starts weeks before an event.

4 weeks to go
- Make sure there is a countdown of days until your travel day in your calendar/planner.

3 weeks to go
- Tweak your training plan now to make sure you avoid heavy power work in the week leading up to the tournament.

2 weeks to go
- Make sure weapons and body/mask cords are working.
- Purchase shelf-stable competition food. Some good examples would be organic jerky and packets of nut butter, but might need to be ordered online, and always allow a few days for shipping.

1 week to go
- Start increasing hydration daily.
- Start to pack regular luggage for the trip.

3 days to go
- Start to increase carbohydrate intake to carb load "gently."
- Have your last intense bouting before the tournament.
- Fence freely, without trying anything new.
- Finish up packing and double check with a list.
- Final check of all weapons and body/mask cords.

2 days to go
- Pack your uniform (including plastron and lame), mask, glove, socks, and fencing shoes **in a carry-on**. Equipment vendors aren't always at tournaments, and these are the pieces that you probably would prefer to not borrow should checked baggage not arrive.

1 day to go
- Check in for your flight.
- Bring a water bottle (fill one or buy one after airport security).
- Bring several small shelf-stable snacks (like trail mix, nuts, nutrition bars), in case you have delays. They happen more than you think.

"The will to win means nothing without the will to prepare."
~ Juma Ikangaa – NYC Marathon winner

PACKING CHECKLIST

Fencing Stuff

- [ ] Fencing Jacket
- [ ] Fencing Pants (aka knickers or breeches)
- [ ] Underarm Protector (aka plastron)
- [ ] Chest Protector
- [ ] Mask
- [ ] 3-6 Weapons
- [ ] 3-6 Body cords
- [ ] 3-6 Mask cords
- [ ] Lamé
- [ ] Backup lamé (if primary one is old)
- [ ] Glove
- [ ] Backup Glove
- [ ] Long Socks (two pairs)
- [ ] Fencing Shoes
- [ ] Flip flops / slides
- [ ] This Journal / Pencils / Post-it Notes

Clothing

- [ ] Shorts (for under uniform)
- [ ] 1-3 Dry fit shirts for pool / DE's
- [ ] Sports Bra (extras if desired)
- [ ] Dry Undergarments (for after tournament)
- [ ] Dry shirt (for after tournament)
- [ ] Club or Team Warm ups / Sweat Suit
- [ ] Dry Socks (for after tournament)
- [ ] Men's Protective Cup
- [ ] Baseball Cap (lights in venues can be overwhelming)

Extras

- [ ] Tightening tools
- [ ] Plastic Bag (for wet clothes)
- [ ] Extra Shoe Laces
- [ ] Water Bottle
- [ ] Electrolyte Powder / Mix-ins
- [ ] Competition Food
- [ ] iPod / phone for music
- [ ] Earbuds / headphones
- [ ] Charging cords and/or battery

FENCING HYDRATION

How much water do I need during competition?
Hydration is a critical element in competition preparedness. *Start the day hydrated!* Hydration for a tournament starts days before! Travel (either by plane or car) can be especially dehydrating. During competition sip moderate amounts (six to eight ounces) of water every fifteen to twenty minutes. In other words, you should drink at least one big water bottle during a round lasting 1-2 hours. Drinking moderately allows your body to absorb the fluid most efficiently. *If you don't have to visit the restroom after your pool, you have not consumed enough water.*

What about sports drinks?
Sports drinks have been touted as contributing the critical difference in an athlete's performance. If fencing were an ultra-endurance sport, that would be true for us. However, there is no advantage for fencers and, in fact, sports drinks can actually dehydrate rather than hydrate if they are the only thing you are drinking. They contain too much sugar and too many electrolytes to be processed efficiently during competition. On the other hand, immediately after competition or heavy training, sports drinks can contribute to your recovery, **but drink them slowly.**

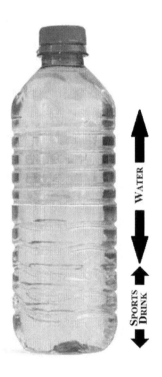

Water is the perfect sports drink. If you have to flavor your water, dilute ¼ to ½ cup of sports drink in a water bottle. If it looks like something that would come out of you, then it is diluted enough. (Provided your favorite flavor is lemon lime!)

During fencing competition: Drink water that is slightly flavored by your favorite sports drink.

After competition or training: Drink a sports drinks, orange juice or non-fat chocolate milk.

GENERAL AND COMPETITION NUTRITION

What is the best diet for an athlete/fencer?
There is a diet that many experts agree is the proper one for athletes:
- 40 to 60% carbohydrates (mostly complex carbs – limit to 10% simple carbs)
- 15 to 25% protein
- 20 to 25% fat – however saturated fat should be no more than 10% of an athlete's diet

There are many great websites and apps to help you figure out if you are meeting these goals.

Eating Breakfast on competition day is vital. What should I eat?
Three to five hours prior to competition:
> 600-calorie meal: simple & complex carbs, protein, a little fat and plenty of water. Example – eggs, potatoes, toast, orange juice, and water. Never forgo your normal caffeine on competition day (equals bad headache).

Fewer than three hours prior to competition:
> 450-calorie meal: Example – One egg, whole-wheat toast, orange juice, and water.

Less than one hour prior to competition:
> "Meal in a can" dietary supplement (with at least 10 grams of protein) and a simpler carb source (ex. fruit)

Most importantly, consume food during pools or immediately after – this isn't a choice. You need to refuel during competition!

Tip – Keep an eye on the time. If you woke up at 6:00AM and it is now 11:00AM your body needs fuel!

Competition food ideas
- Bananas, apples, oranges, watermelon, cucumbers
- Fig Newtons, low fat crackers
- Cheese sticks, nut butter, soy butter, sunflower butter
- Bagels, whole grain bread, rice cakes (but be careful – one bagel equals 4 slices of bread!)
- Baby carrots, snap peas, string beans, edamame
- Dried apricots, raisins, dried cranberries, almonds, cashews, walnuts, or trail mix
- Granola bars, Luna® bars, Clif® bars, Kind® bars

POOL SCORESHEET (SAMPLE)

Tournament: November SYC **Date:** 11/24/2017

Name	1	2	3	4	5	6	7	V	TS	TR	Ind
1 Johnson, Charlie (GFC)		V	V	V	V	V	4	5	29	13	+16
2 Smith, Adam (FC)	1		V	V	1	V	1	3	18	24	-6
3 Harris, Ed (Masters)	2	3		V	V	V	0	3	20	26	-6
4 Jones, Bill (FAP)	1	4	4		V	V	4	2	23	25	-2
5 Warner, George A. (FC)	3	V	3	3		V	3	2	22	22	0
6 Clinton, Frank (ST)	1	2	4	2	1		3	0	13	30	-17
7 Lee, Dennis (Forte)	V	V	V	V	V	V		6	30	15	+15

Referees: Jane Smith, Steve Richards

QUICK SCOUTING OF MY POOL (SAMPLE)

Name: Johnson V-4 Righty/**Lefty**	**Name:** Clinton V-3 **Righty**/Lefty
Favorite Attack: bait 4 3 blade take	**Favorite Attack:** Simple attack off line
Favorite Defense: circle 3	**Favorite Defense:** Big 2 (sloppy)
Actions I think will work: FD around circle 3 Composed attack in prep	**Actions I think will work:** Pull distance new fencer- nice kid- FD around 2 work- hard to hit
Name: Smith V-1 **Righty**/Lefty	**Name:** Warner V-3 **Righty**/Lefty
Favorite Attack: Beat 4 attack	**Favorite Attack:** FD 4 to 3 / 4 to flank
Favorite Defense: sweep 5	**Favorite Defense:** beat 4 / sweep 4 PR
Actions I think will work: FD 5 to flank PR 3 beat attack	**Actions I think will work:** FD- former epeeist??? Watch arm for stop cut
Name: Harris V-0 **Righty**/Lefty	**Name:** Jones V-4 **Righty**/Lefty
Favorite Attack: Quick off the line	**Favorite Attack:** big steps and wild blade take
Favorite Defense: 4	**Favorite Defense:** BIG circle 5 (sloppy)
Actions I think will work: Pull distance Line then PR	**Actions I think will work:** FD to arm avoid blade - strong wild blade takes. Try to push
Top 3 touches from pool:	**Notes about this pool:**
Did take false parry real parry several times.	Ask Coach about endurance - got tired easily
Pulled distance and kept balance	Finally beat Johnson after all these years!!!
Set up actions - had a plan that worked!! Yay!	Maybe I should ask for crossover judges vs Clinton

DIRECT ELIMINATION SCORESHEET (SAMPLE W/ASSISTANCE)

Direct Elimination	Tournament: November SYC																												Date: 11/24/2017		
Table of: 32	(yellow card)							red card										black card										video ☐		V/D	score
seed	Name/Club	1	2	3	4	5	6	7	8	9	1 0	1 1	1 2	1 3	1 4	1 5	1 6	1 7	1 8	1 9	2 0	2 1	2 2	2 3	2 4	2 5	2 6	2 7	2 8	2 9		
4	Me	1	2	3				4	5	6	7	8	9	1 0	1 1																V	5
5	Smith, J (FC)	1	2	3								1 2	3	4	5																D	4

	yellow card	red card	black card	video ☐	

Referee: Steve Richards

Actions that worked:
Attacks with confidence. Changing tempo of push.

Actions that did not:
any actions that I hesitated.

Actions to try next time:
actions with smaller steps and full confidence.

Notes:
Felt like I needed more time to prepare for the bout. Next time I will eat right after the pool. And do jogging in place and some advance lunges prior to the bout.

DIRECT ELIMINATION SCORESHEET (SAMPLE BY YOURSELF)

Direct Elimination	Tournament: November SYC																													Date: 11/24/2017		
Table of: 32	**(yellow card)**									red card										black card									video ☐		
seed	Name/Club	1	2	3	4	5	6	7	8	9	1 0	1 1	1 2	1 3	1 4	1 5	1 6	1 7	1 8	1 9	2 0	2 1	2 2	2 3	2 4	2 5	2 6	2 7	2 8	2 9	score	V/D
4	Me																														5	V
5	Smith, J (FC)																														4	D

yellow card   red card   black card   video ☐

Referee: Steve Richards

Actions that worked:
Attacks with confidence. Changing tempo of push.

Actions that did not:
Any actions that I hesitated.

Actions to try next time:
actions with smaller steps and full confidence.

Notes:
Felt like I needed more time to prepare for the bout. Next time I will eat right after the pool. And do jogging in place and some advance lunges prior to the bout.

TOURNAMENT EVALUATION (SAMPLE)

Tournament: November SYC   **Date:** 11/24/2017

Energy Level	Fatigued	Full of energy	
How did I feel today?	1 2 3 4 5 6 **7** 8 9 10		
Performance Level	Poor	Wow! I kick butt!	
How did I feel today?	1 2 3 4 5 6 **7** 8 9 10		
Competition Eval.	Little	A lot	
Concentration Level:	1 2 3 4 **5** 6 7 8 9 10		
Intensity Level:	1 2 3 4 5 **6** 7 8 9 10		
Relaxation Level:	1 2 3 **4** 5 6 7 8 9 10		
General Fulfillment:	1 2 3 4 5 **6** 7 8 9 10		
	Poor	Excellent	
Bladework skills:	1 2 3 4 **5** 6 7 8 9 10		
Footwork skills:	1 2 3 4 5 **6** 7 8 9 10		

Great Job! Believe in yourself! Keep Working!

10 Things I need to work on:
1. Almost overslept- stressed me out the whole day.
2. Blade control not precise for pool- better in DE's
3. Distance- too far, not finishing at the correct moment.
4. Got stubborn- tried to force actions
5. Felt rushed for DE- took a few touches to get it together.
6. Had trouble with the new-ish fencer in pool
7. Confidence on a good action or plan.
8. Going around circular defense.
9. Integrating lessons into competition bouts- I am scared to.
10. Felt super tired for last DE.

10 Solutions to those things:
1. Set two alarms. Practice the relaxation stuff from camp
2. Target work more at club. More warm up for pools-maybe
3. Probably need smaller steps like Coach always tells me. Vary speed of push.
4. If I feel stuck - take a breath and try to think tactically.
5. Keep better track of time after pools finish.
6. Ask Coach about fencing new people and what to do.
7. Try and find the mind set to believe in myself
8. Ask a teammate to do only circular defense at club (drills?)
9. Find moments in bout that are like lessons and DO IT!
10. Didn't eat enough during day - Coach says I need more fuel.

TOURNAMENT EVALUATION (PAGE 2 SAMPLE)

10 Things I did well:
1. Ate breakfast in spite of waking a little late.
2. Had a really good feint deceive in bout versus FC fencer.
3. re-warm up for DE better than pools.
4. developed an long feint deceive attack. (in a couple of bouts)
5. Was brave and asked referee to quiet a too loud coach/parent.
6. Calmly handled equipment having issues (blade broke - cord).
7. Beat the lefty in the pool. Need more work with them though.
8. stayed to watch fencer who beat me to get ideas for next time.
9. Cheered on teammates during DE's
10. Drank enough water and sports drink.

Need to ask my coach:
1. About fencing sloppy/ new fencers.
2. how to apply actions into bout- (distance and timing)
3. How to believe in myself more.
4.
5.
6.
7.
8.
9.
10.

Do I need to change my current training plan? How?
Coach thinks I got tired because of eating, maybe I need to work on my endurance too.
How? I will build up my footwork times when practicing.

"The will to win means nothing without the will to prepare."
~Juma Ikangaa, NYC Marathon winner

POOL BOUT ORDERS

POOL OF 5	POOL OF 6	POOL OF 7	POOL OF 8
1-2	1-2	1-4	2-3
3-4	4-3	2-5	1-5
5-1	6-5	3-6	7-4
2-3	3-1	7-1	6-8
5-4	2-6	5-4	1-2
1-3	5-4	2-3	3-4
2-5	1-6	6-7	5-6
4-1	3-5	5-1	8-7
3-5	4-2	4-3	4-1
4-2	5-1	6-2	5-2
	6-4	5-7	8-3
	2-3	3-1	6-7
	1-4	4-6	4-2
	5-2	7-2	8-1
	3-6	3-5	7-5
		1-6	3-6
		2-4	2-8
		7-3	5-4
		6-5	6-1
		1-2	3-7
		4-7	4-8
			2-6
			3-5
			1-7
			4-6
			8-5
			7-2
			1-3

POOL NUMBER

Tournament Name	Tournament Date	Today my number in the pool is
November SYC	11/24/2017	7

POOL SCORESHEET

Tournament: | **Date:**

Name	1	2	3	4	5	6	7	V	TS	TR	Ind
1											
2											
3											
4											
5											
6											
7											

Referees:

20

QUICK SCOUTING OF MY POOL

Name:	Righty/Lefty	Name:	Righty/Lefty
Favorite Attack:		Favorite Attack:	
Favorite Defense:		Favorite Defense:	
Actions I think will work:		Actions I think will work:	
Name:	Righty/Lefty	Name:	Righty/Lefty
Favorite Attack:		Favorite Attack:	
Favorite Defense:		Favorite Defense:	
Actions I think will work:		Actions I think will work:	
Name:	Righty/Lefty	Name:	Righty/Lefty
Favorite Attack:		Favorite Attack:	
Favorite Defense:		Favorite Defense:	
Actions I think will work:		Actions I think will work:	
Top 3 touches from pool:		Notes about this pool:	

DIRECT ELIMINATION SCORESHEET

Direct Elimination	Tournament:																													Date:	
Table of:		yellow card								red card									black card										video ☐	V/D	
Name/Club		1	2	3	4	5	6	7	8	9	10	11	12	13	14	15	16	17	18	19	20	21	22	23	24	25	26	27	28	29	score
seed																															
		yellow card								red card									black card										video ☐		

Referee:

Actions that worked:
_____
_____

Actions that did not:
_____
_____

Actions to try next time:
_____
_____

Notes:
_____
_____

DIRECT ELIMINATION SCORESHEET

Direct Elimination	Tournament:																					Date:	
Table of:	yellow card									red card				black card							video ☐	V/D	
Name/ Club	1	2	3	4	5	6	7	8	9	10	11	12	13	14	15	16	17	18	19	20	21	22	score
seed																								
	yellow card									red card				black card							video ☐		

Referee:

Actions that worked:

Actions that did not:

Actions to try next time:

Notes:

DIRECT ELIMINATION SCORESHEET

Direct Elimination	Tournament:																											Date:	
Table of:	yellow card								red card										black card									video ☐	V/D
	1	2	3	4	5	6	7	8	9	10	11	12	13	14	15	16	17	18	19	20	21	22	23	24	25	26	27	28	29	score
Name/ Club																														
	yellow card								red card										black card									video ☐	
seed																														

Referee:

Actions that worked:

Actions that did not:

Actions to try next time:

Notes:

DIRECT ELIMINATION SCORESHEET

Direct Elimination	Tournament:																								Date:	
Table of:	yellow card								red card					black card									video ☐		V/D	
																									score	
Name/ Club	1	2	3	4	5	6	7	8	9	1 0	1 1	1 2	1 3	1 4	1 5	1 6	1 7	1 8	1 9	2 0	2 1	2 2	2 3	2 4	2 5	
seed																										
	yellow card					red card					black card													video ☐		

Referee:

Actions that worked:

Actions that did not:

Actions to try next time:

Notes:

DIRECT ELIMINATION SCORESHEET

Direct Elimination	Tournament:																													Date:	
Table of:	yellow card								red card											black card									video ☐	V/D
Name/ Club	1	2	3	4	5	6	7	8	9	10	11	12	13	14	15	16	17	18	19	20	21	22	23	24	25	26	27	28	29	score
seed																															
	yellow card								red card											black card									video ☐	

Referee:

Actions that worked:

Actions that did not:

Actions to try next time:

Notes:

DIRECT ELIMINATION SCORESHEET

Direct Elimination	Tournament:																				Date:		
Table of:	yellow card								red card				black card								video ☐	score	V/D
	1	2	3	4	5	6	7	8	9	10	11	12	13	14	15	16	17	18	19	20	21	22	
Name/ Club																							
seed																							
	yellow card								red card				black card								video ☐		

Referee:

Actions that worked:

Actions that did not:

Actions to try next time:

Notes:

TOURNAMENT EVALUATION

Tournament:	Date:

Energy Level	Fatigued　　　Full of energy	
How did I feel today?	1 2 3 4 5 6 7 8 9 10	
Performance Level	Poor　　　Wow! I kick butt!	Great Job! Believe in yourself! Keep Working!
How did I feel today?	1 2 3 4 5 6 7 8 9 10	
Competition Eval.	Little　　　　　　　A lot!	
Concentration Level:	1 2 3 4 5 6 7 8 9 10	
Intensity Level:	1 2 3 4 5 6 7 8 9 10	
Relaxation Level:	1 2 3 4 5 6 7 8 9 10	
General Fulfillment:	1 2 3 4 5 6 7 8 9 10	
	Poor　　　　　　　Excellent	
Bladework skills:	1 2 3 4 5 6 7 8 9 10	
Footwork skills:	1 2 3 4 5 6 7 8 9 10	

10 Things I need to work on:

1.
2.
3.
4.
5.
6.
7.
8.
9.
10.

10 Solutions to those things:

1.
2.
3.
4.
5.
6.
7.
8.
9.
10.

TOURNAMENT EVALUATION (PAGE 2)

10 Things I did well:
1.
2.
3.
4.
5.
6.
7.
8.
9.
10.

Need to ask my coach:
1.
2.
3.
4.
5.
6.
7.
8.
9.
10.

Do I need to change my current training plan? How?

"The will to win means nothing without the will to prepare."
~Juma Ikangaa, NYC Marathon winner

POOL SCORESHEET

Tournament: **Date:**

Name	1	2	3	4	5	6	7	V	TS	TR	Ind
1											
2											
3											
4											
5											
6											
7											

Referees:

QUICK SCOUTING OF MY POOL

Name:	Righty/Lefty	Name:	Righty/Lefty
Favorite Attack:		Favorite Attack:	
Favorite Defense:		Favorite Defense:	
Actions I think will work:		Actions I think will work:	
Name:	Righty/Lefty	Name:	Righty/Lefty
Favorite Attack:		Favorite Attack:	
Favorite Defense:		Favorite Defense:	
Actions I think will work:		Actions I think will work:	
Name:	Righty/Lefty	Name:	Righty/Lefty
Favorite Attack:		Favorite Attack:	
Favorite Defense:		Favorite Defense:	
Actions I think will work:		Actions I think will work:	
Top 3 touches from pool:		Notes about this pool:	

DIRECT ELIMINATION SCORESHEET

Direct Elimination	Tournament:																													Date:	
Table of:	yellow card ☐									red card										black card									video ☐	V/D	
																														score	
Name/Club	1	2	3	4	5	6	7	8	9	10	11	12	13	14	15	16	17	18	19	20	21	22	23	24	25	26	27	28	29		
seed																															

yellow card ☐   red card   black card   video ☐

Referee:

Actions that worked:

Actions that did not:

Actions to try next time:

Notes:

DIRECT ELIMINATION SCORESHEET

Direct Elimination	Tournament:																						Date:		
Table of:	yellow card									red card					black card							video ☐		V/D
																								score
Name/Club	1	2	3	4	5	6	7	8	9	1 0	1 1	1 2	1 3	1 4	1 5	1 6	1 7	1 8	1 9	2 0	2 1	2 2	2 3	2 4	2 5	2 6	2 7	2 8	2 9		
seed																								

	yellow card	red card	black card	video ☐

Referee:

Actions that worked:

Actions that did not:

Actions to try next time:

Notes:

DIRECT ELIMINATION SCORESHEET

Direct Elimination	Tournament:				Date:	

Table of:		yellow card	red card	black card	video ☐	V/D
						score
Name/Club		1 2 3 4 5 6 7 8 9	1 1 1 1 0 1 2 3	1 1 1 1 1 1 4 5 6 7 8 9	2 2 2 2 2 2 2 2 2 2 0 1 2 3 4 5 6 7 8 9	
seed						

	yellow card	red card	black card	video ☐

Referee:

Actions that worked:

Actions that did not:

Actions to try next time:

Notes:

DIRECT ELIMINATION SCORESHEET

Direct Elimination	Tournament:																								Date:		
Table of:	yellow card								red card									black card							video ☐	score	V/D
Name/Club	1	2	3	4	5	6	7	8	9	10	11	12	13	14	15	16	17	18	19	20	21	22	23	24	25		
seed																											
	yellow card								red card									black card							video ☐		

Referee:

Actions that worked:

Actions that did not:

Actions to try next time:

Notes:

DIRECT ELIMINATION SCORESHEET

Direct Elimination	Tournament:																													Date:	
Table of:	yellow card									red card										black card									video ☐	V/D	
Name/Club	1	2	3	4	5	6	7	8	9	10	11	12	13	14	15	16	17	18	19	20	21	22	23	24	25	26	27	28	29	score	
seed																															
	yellow card									red card										black card									video ☐		

Referee:

Actions that worked:

Actions that did not:

Actions to try next time:

Notes:

DIRECT ELIMINATION SCORESHEET

Direct Elimination	Tournament:																													Date:	
Table of:	yellow card								red card						black card											video ☐				V/D	
Name/ Club	1	2	3	4	5	6	7	8	9	10	11	12	13	14	15	16	17	18	19	20	21	22	23	24	25	26	27	28	29	score	
seed																															

yellow card   red card   black card   video ☐

Referee:

Actions that worked:

Actions that did not:

Actions to try next time:

Notes:

TOURNAMENT EVALUATION

Tournament:	Date:

Energy Level	Fatigued	Full of energy
How did I feel today?	*1 2 3 4 5 6 7 8 9 10*	
Performance Level	Poor	Wow! I kick butt!
How did I feel today?	*1 2 3 4 5 6 7 8 9 10*	
Competition Eval.	Little	A lot!
Concentration Level:	*1 2 3 4 5 6 7 8 9 10*	
Intensity Level:	*1 2 3 4 5 6 7 8 9 10*	
Relaxation Level:	*1 2 3 4 5 6 7 8 9 10*	
General Fulfillment:	*1 2 3 4 5 6 7 8 9 10*	
	Poor	Excellent
Bladework skills:	*1 2 3 4 5 6 7 8 9 10*	
Footwork skills:	*1 2 3 4 5 6 7 8 9 10*	

Great Job! Believe in yourself! Keep Working!

10 Things I need to work on:
1.
2.
3.
4.
5.
6.
7.
8.
9.
10.

10 Solutions to those things:
1.
2.
3.
4.
5.
6.
7.
8.
9.
10.

TOURNAMENT EVALUATION (PAGE 2)

10 Things I did well:
1.
2.
3.
4.
5.
6.
7.
8.
9.
10.

Need to ask my coach:
1.
2.
3.
4.
5.
6.
7.
8.
9.
10.

Do I need to change my current training plan? How?

"The will to win means nothing without the will to prepare."
~Juma Ikangaa, NYC Marathon winner

POOL SCORESHEET

Tournament: **Date:**

Name	1	2	3	4	5	6	7	V	TS	TR	Ind
1											
2											
3											
4											
5											
6											
7											

Referees:

QUICK SCOUTING OF MY POOL

Name:	Righty/Lefty	Name:	Righty/Lefty
Favorite Attack:		Favorite Attack:	
Favorite Defense:		Favorite Defense:	
Actions I think will work:		Actions I think will work:	

Name:	Righty/Lefty	Name:	Righty/Lefty
Favorite Attack:		Favorite Attack:	
Favorite Defense:		Favorite Defense:	
Actions I think will work:		Actions I think will work:	

Name:	Righty/Lefty	Name:	Righty/Lefty
Favorite Attack:		Favorite Attack:	
Favorite Defense:		Favorite Defense:	
Actions I think will work:		Actions I think will work:	

Top 3 touches from pool:	Notes about this pool:

DIRECT ELIMINATION SCORESHEET

Direct Elimination	Tournament:																								Date:	
Table of:	yellow card									red card									black card						video ☐	V/D
																										score
Name/ Club	1	2	3	4	5	6	7	8	9	1 0	1 1	1 2	1 3	1 4	1 5	1 6	1 7	1 8	1 9	2 0	2 1	2 2	2 3	2 4	2 5	
																									2 6 2 7 2 8 2 9	
seed	yellow card									red card									black card						video ☐	

Referee:

Actions that worked:

Actions that did not:

Actions to try next time:

Notes:

DIRECT ELIMINATION SCORESHEET

Direct Elimination	Tournament:																								Date:		
Table of:	yellow card									red card					black card									video ☐		V/D	
																										score	
Name/Club	1	2	3	4	5	6	7	8	9	1 0	1 1	1 2	1 3	1 4	1 5	1 6	1 7	1 8	1 9	2 0	2 1	2 2	2 3	2 4	2 5		
seed																											
	yellow card					red card					black card													video ☐			

Referee:

Actions that worked:

Actions that did not:

Actions to try next time:

Notes:

DIRECT ELIMINATION SCORESHEET

Direct Elimination	Tournament:																											Date:	
Table of:	yellow card									red card									black card									video ☐	V/D
Name/Club	1	2	3	4	5	6	7	8	9	10	11	12	13	14	15	16	17	18	19	20	21	22	23	24	25	26	27	28	29	score
	yellow card									red card									black card									video ☐	
seed																														

Referee:

Actions that worked:

Actions that did not:

Actions to try next time:

Notes:

DIRECT ELIMINATION SCORESHEET

Direct Elimination	Tournament:																							Date:			
Table of:	yellow card									red card										black card					video ☐		V/D
	1	2	3	4	5	6	7	8	9	10	11	12	13	14	15	16	17	18	19	20	21	22	23	24	25	26	27	28	29	score
Name/Club																											
seed																											
	yellow card									red card										black card					video ☐		

Referee:

Actions that worked:

Actions that did not:

Actions to try next time:

Notes:

DIRECT ELIMINATION SCORESHEET

Direct Elimination	Tournament:																												Date:	
Table of:	yellow card									red card										black card									video ☐	V/D
Name/ Club	1	2	3	4	5	6	7	8	9	1 0	1 1	1 2	1 3	1 4	1 5	1 6	1 7	1 8	1 9	2 0	2 1	2 2	2 3	2 4	2 5	2 6	2 7	2 8	2 9	score
seed																														
	yellow card									red card										black card									video ☐	

Referee:

Actions that worked:

Actions that did not:

Actions to try next time:

Notes:

DIRECT ELIMINATION SCORESHEET

Direct Elimination	Tournament:																													Date:	
Table of:	yellow card							red card									black card											video ☐		V/D	
Name/ Club	1	2	3	4	5	6	7	8	9	10	11	12	13	14	15	16	17	18	19	20	21	22	23	24	25	26	27	28	29	score
	yellow card							red card									black card											video ☐			
seed																															

Referee:

Actions that worked:

Actions that did not:

Actions to try next time:

Notes:

TOURNAMENT EVALUATION

Tournament:	Date:

Energy Level	Fatigued	Full of energy	
How did I feel today?	1 2 3 4 5 6 7 8 9 10		
Performance Level	Poor	Wow! I kick butt!	
How did I feel today?	1 2 3 4 5 6 7 8 9 10		
Competition Eval.	Little	A lot!	Great Job! Believe in yourself! Keep Working!
Concentration Level:	1 2 3 4 5 6 7 8 9 10		
Intensity Level:	1 2 3 4 5 6 7 8 9 10		
Relaxation Level:	1 2 3 4 5 6 7 8 9 10		
General Fulfillment:	1 2 3 4 5 6 7 8 9 10		
	Poor	Excellent	
Bladework skills:	1 2 3 4 5 6 7 8 9 10		
Footwork skills:	1 2 3 4 5 6 7 8 9 10		

10 Things I need to work on:
1.
2.
3.
4.
5.
6.
7.
8.
9.
10.

10 Solutions to those things:
1.
2.
3.
4.
5.
6.
7.
8.
9.
10.

TOURNAMENT EVALUATION (PAGE 2)

10 Things I did well:
1.
2.
3.
4.
5.
6.
7.
8.
9.
10.

Need to ask my coach:
1.
2.
3.
4.
5.
6.
7.
8.
9.
10.

Do I need to change my current training plan? How?

"The will to win means nothing without the will to prepare."
~Juma Ikangaa, NYC Marathon winner

POOL SCORESHEET

Tournament: **Date:**

Name	1	2	3	4	5	6	7	V	TS	TR	Ind
1											
2											
3											
4											
5											
6											
7											

Referees:

QUICK SCOUTING OF MY POOL

Name: Righty/Lefty	Name: Righty/Lefty
Favorite Attack:	Favorite Attack:
Favorite Defense:	Favorite Defense:
Actions I think will work:	Actions I think will work:
Name: Righty/Lefty	Name: Righty/Lefty
Favorite Attack:	Favorite Attack:
Favorite Defense:	Favorite Defense:
Actions I think will work:	Actions I think will work:
Name: Righty/Lefty	Name: Righty/Lefty
Favorite Attack:	Favorite Attack:
Favorite Defense:	Favorite Defense:
Actions I think will work:	Actions I think will work:
Top 3 touches from pool:	Notes about this pool:

DIRECT ELIMINATION SCORESHEET

Direct Elimination	Tournament:																												Date:	
Table of:	yellow card								red card										black card										video ☐	
Name/ Club	1	2	3	4	5	6	7	8	9	10	11	12	13	14	15	16	17	18	19	20	21	22	23	24	25	26	27	28	29	score
																														V/D
seed																														
	yellow card								red card										black card										video ☐	

Referee:

Actions that worked:

Actions that did not:

Actions to try next time:

Notes:

DIRECT ELIMINATION SCORESHEET

Direct Elimination	Tournament:		Date:	
Table of:	yellow card / red card / black card	video ☐	V/D score	
Name/ Club	1 2 3 4 5 6 7 8 9 10 11 12 13 14 15 16 17 18 19 20 21 22 23 24 25 26 27 28 29			
seed				
	yellow card / red card / black card	video ☐		

Referee:

Actions that worked:

Actions that did not:

Actions to try next time:

Notes:

DIRECT ELIMINATION SCORESHEET

Direct Elimination	Tournament:																												Date:	
Table of:	yellow card									red card										black card									video ☐	V/D
	1	2	3	4	5	6	7	8	9	10	11	12	13	14	15	16	17	18	19	20	21	22	23	24	25	26	27	28	29	score
Name/ Club																														
seed																														
	yellow card									red card										black card									video ☐	

Referee:

Actions that worked:

Actions that did not:

Actions to try next time:

Notes:

DIRECT ELIMINATION SCORESHEET

Direct Elimination	Tournament:																						Date:		
Table of:	yellow card									red card										black card				video ☐	V/D
	1	2	3	4	5	6	7	8	9	10	11	12	13	14	15	16	17	18	19	20	21	22	23		score
Name/Club																									
seed																									
	yellow card									red card										black card				video ☐	

Referee:

Actions that worked:

Actions that did not:

Actions to try next time:

Notes:

DIRECT ELIMINATION SCORESHEET

Direct Elimination	Tournament:																											Date:	
Table of:	yellow card								red card										black card									video ☐	V/D
	1	2	3	4	5	6	7	8	9	10	11	12	13	14	15	16	17	18	19	20	21	22	23	24	25	26	27	28	score
Name/ Club																													
seed																													
	yellow card								red card										black card									video ☐	

Referee:

Actions that worked:

Actions that did not:

Actions to try next time:

Notes:

DIRECT ELIMINATION SCORESHEET

Direct Elimination	Tournament:																													Date:		
Table of:	yellow card								red card										black card										video ☐		V/D	
																															score	
Name/Club	1	2	3	4	5	6	7	8	9	1 0	1 1	1 2	1 3	1 4	1 5	1 6	1 7	1 8	1 9	2 0	2 1	2 2	2 3	2 4	2 5	2 6	2 7	2 8	2 9			
seed																																
	yellow card								red card										black card										video ☐			

Referee:

Actions that worked:

Actions that did not:

Actions to try next time:

Notes:

TOURNAMENT EVALUATION

Tournament:	Date:

Energy Level	Fatigued	Full of energy
How did I feel today?	1 2 3 4 5 6 7 8 9 10	
Performance Level	Poor	Wow! I kick butt!
How did I feel today?	1 2 3 4 5 6 7 8 9 10	
Competition Eval.	Little	A lot!
Concentration Level:	1 2 3 4 5 6 7 8 9 10	
Intensity Level:	1 2 3 4 5 6 7 8 9 10	
Relaxation Level:	1 2 3 4 5 6 7 8 9 10	
General Fulfillment:	1 2 3 4 5 6 7 8 9 10	
	Poor	Excellent
Bladework skills:	1 2 3 4 5 6 7 8 9 10	
Footwork skills:	1 2 3 4 5 6 7 8 9 10	

Great Job! Believe in yourself! Keep Working!

10 Things I need to work on:
1.
2.
3.
4.
5.
6.
7.
8.
9.
10.

10 Solutions to those things:
1.
2.
3.
4.
5.
6.
7.
8.
9.
10.

TOURNAMENT EVALUATION (PAGE 2)

10 Things I did well:
1.
2.
3.
4.
5.
6.
7.
8.
9.
10.

Need to ask my coach:
1.
2.
3.
4.
5.
6.
7.
8.
9.
10.

Do I need to change my current training plan? How?

"The will to win means nothing without the will to prepare."
~Juma Ikangaa, NYC Marathon winner

POOL SCORESHEET

Tournament: **Date:**

Name	1	2	3	4	5	6	7	V	TS	TR	Ind
1											
2											
3											
4											
5											
6											
7											

Referees:

QUICK SCOUTING OF MY POOL

Name:	Righty/Lefty	Name:	Righty/Lefty
Favorite Attack:		Favorite Attack:	
Favorite Defense:		Favorite Defense:	
Actions I think will work:		Actions I think will work:	
Name:	Righty/Lefty	Name:	Righty/Lefty
Favorite Attack:		Favorite Attack:	
Favorite Defense:		Favorite Defense:	
Actions I think will work:		Actions I think will work:	
Name:	Righty/Lefty	Name:	Righty/Lefty
Favorite Attack:		Favorite Attack:	
Favorite Defense:		Favorite Defense:	
Actions I think will work:		Actions I think will work:	
Top 3 touches from pool:		Notes about this pool:	

DIRECT ELIMINATION SCORESHEET

Direct Elimination	Tournament:																													Date:	
Table of:	yellow card								red card											black card									video ☐		V/D
																															score
Name/Club	1	2	3	4	5	6	7	8	9	1 0	1 1	1 2	1 3	1 4	1 5	1 6	1 7	1 8	1 9	2 0	2 1	2 2	2 3	2 4	2 5	2 6	2 7	2 8	2 9	
seed																															

	yellow card	red card	black card	video ☐

Referee:

Actions that worked:

Actions that did not:

Actions to try next time:

Notes:

DIRECT ELIMINATION SCORESHEET

Direct Elimination	Tournament:																					Date:	
Table of:	yellow card									red card					black card						video ☐	V/D	
Name/Club	1	2	3	4	5	6	7	8	9	10	11	12	13	14	15	16	17	18	19	20	21	22	score
seed																							
	yellow card									red card					black card						video ☐		

Referee:

Actions that worked:

Actions that did not:

Actions to try next time:

Notes:

DIRECT ELIMINATION SCORESHEET

Direct Elimination	Tournament:																								Date:	
Table of:	yellow card									red card										black card					video ☐	☐
	1	2	3	4	5	6	7	8	9	10	11	12	13	14	15	16	17	18	19	20	21	22	23	24	25	26	27	28	29	V/D
Name/Club																														score
seed																														
	yellow card									red card										black card					video ☐	☐

Referee:

Actions that worked:

Actions that did not:

Actions to try next time:

Notes:

DIRECT ELIMINATION SCORESHEET

Direct Elimination	Tournament:																													Date:	
Table of:	yellow card									red card										black card										video ☐	V/D
	1	2	3	4	5	6	7	8	9	10	11	12	13	14	15	16	17	18	19	20	21	22	23	24	25	26	27	28	29		score
Name/Club																															
seed																															
	yellow card									red card										black card										video ☐	

Referee:

Actions that worked:

Actions that did not:

Actions to try next time:

Notes:

DIRECT ELIMINATION SCORESHEET

Direct Elimination	Tournament:																						Date:		
Table of:	yellow card								red card							black card								video ☐	V/D
	1	2	3	4	5	6	7	8	9	10	11	12	13	14	15	16	17	18	19	20	21	22	23	24	score
Name/ Club																									
seed																									
	yellow card								red card							black card								video ☐	

Referee:

Actions that worked:

Actions that did not:

Actions to try next time:

Notes:

DIRECT ELIMINATION SCORESHEET

Direct Elimination	Tournament:																			Date:	
Table of:	yellow card								red card						black card					video ☐	V/D
Name/Club	1	2	3	4	5	6	7	8	9	10	11	12	13	14	15	16	17	18	19		score
seed																					
	yellow card								red card						black card					video ☐	

Referee:

Actions that worked:

Actions that did not:

Actions to try next time:

Notes:

TOURNAMENT EVALUATION

Tournament: **Date:**

Energy Level	Fatigued	Full of energy
How did I feel today?	*1 2 3 4 5 6 7 8 9 10*	
Performance Level	Poor	Wow! I kick butt!
How did I feel today?	*1 2 3 4 5 6 7 8 9 10*	
Competition Eval.	Little	A lot!
Concentration Level:	*1 2 3 4 5 6 7 8 9 10*	
Intensity Level:	*1 2 3 4 5 6 7 8 9 10*	
Relaxation Level:	*1 2 3 4 5 6 7 8 9 10*	
General Fulfillment:	*1 2 3 4 5 6 7 8 9 10*	
	Poor	Excellent
Bladework skills:	*1 2 3 4 5 6 7 8 9 10*	
Footwork skills:	*1 2 3 4 5 6 7 8 9 10*	

Great Job! Believe in yourself! Keep Working!

10 Things I need to work on:

1.
2.
3.
4.
5.
6.
7.
8.
9.
10.

10 Solutions to those things:

1.
2.
3.
4.
5.
6.
7.
8.
9.
10.

TOURNAMENT EVALUATION (PAGE 2)

10 Things I did well:
1.
2.
3.
4.
5.
6.
7.
8.
9.
10.

Need to ask my coach:
1.
2.
3.
4.
5.
6.
7.
8.
9.
10.

Do I need to change my current training plan? How?

"The will to win means nothing without the will to prepare."
~Juma Ikangaa, NYC Marathon winner

POOL SCORESHEET

Tournament: **Date:**

Name	1	2	3	4	5	6	7	V	TS	TR	Ind
1											
2											
3											
4											
5											
6											
7											

Referees:

QUICK SCOUTING OF MY POOL

Name:	Righty/Lefty	Name:	Righty/Lefty
Favorite Attack:		Favorite Attack:	
Favorite Defense:		Favorite Defense:	
Actions I think will work:		Actions I think will work:	
Name:	Righty/Lefty	Name:	Righty/Lefty
Favorite Attack:		Favorite Attack:	
Favorite Defense:		Favorite Defense:	
Actions I think will work:		Actions I think will work:	
Name:	Righty/Lefty	Name:	Righty/Lefty
Favorite Attack:		Favorite Attack:	
Favorite Defense:		Favorite Defense:	
Actions I think will work:		Actions I think will work:	
Top 3 touches from pool:		Notes about this pool:	

DIRECT ELIMINATION SCORESHEET

Direct Elimination	Tournament:																													Date:	
Table of:	yellow card								red card										black card										video ☐		
Name/Club	1	2	3	4	5	6	7	8	9	10	11	12	13	14	15	16	17	18	19	20	21	22	23	24	25	26	27	28	29	V/D	
																															score
seed																															
	yellow card								red card										black card										video ☐	

Referee:

Actions that worked:

Actions that did not:

Actions to try next time:

Notes:

DIRECT ELIMINATION SCORESHEET

Direct Elimination	Tournament:																					Date:	
Table of:	yellow card								red card									black card				video ☐	score
	1	2	3	4	5	6	7	8	9	10	11	12	13	14	15	16	17	18	19	20	21	22	V/D
Name/Club																							
seed																							
	yellow card								red card									black card				video ☐	

Referee:

Actions that worked:

Actions that did not:

Actions to try next time:

Notes:

DIRECT ELIMINATION SCORESHEET

Direct Elimination	Tournament:																													Date:	
Table of:	yellow card ☐									red card									black card										video ☐	V/D	
																														score	
Name/Club	1	2	3	4	5	6	7	8	9	10	11	12	13	14	15	16	17	18	19	20	21	22	23	24	25	26	27	28	29		
seed																																
	yellow card			red card			black card		video ☐		

Referee:

Actions that worked:

Actions that did not:

Actions to try next time:

Notes:

DIRECT ELIMINATION SCORESHEET

Direct Elimination	Tournament:																												Date:	
Table of:	yellow card									red card										black card									video ☐	V/D
Name/ Club	1	2	3	4	5	6	7	8	9	10	11	12	13	14	15	16	17	18	19	20	21	22	23	24	25	26	27	28	29	score
seed																														
	yellow card									red card										black card									video ☐	

Referee:

Actions that worked:

Actions that did not:

Actions to try next time:

Notes:

DIRECT ELIMINATION SCORESHEET

Direct Elimination	Tournament:																									Date:		
Table of:	yellow card									red card									black card								video ☐	V/D
	1	2	3	4	5	6	7	8	9	10	11	12	13	14	15	16	17	18	19	20	21	22	23	24	25	26	27	28	29	score
Name/Club																														
seed																														

	yellow card	red card	black card	video ☐

Referee:

Actions that worked:

Actions that did not:

Actions to try next time:

Notes:

DIRECT ELIMINATION SCORESHEET

Direct Elimination	Tournament:																			Date:		
Table of:	yellow card							red card					black card						video ☐	V/D	
	1	2	3	4	5	6	7	8	9	10	11	12	13	14	15	16	17	18	19		score
Name/Club																					
seed																					

	yellow card	red card	black card	video ☐

Referee:

Actions that worked:

Actions that did not:

Actions to try next time:

Notes:

TOURNAMENT EVALUATION

Tournament:	Date:

Energy Level	Fatigued	Full of energy
How did I feel today?	*1 2 3 4 5 6 7 8 9 10*	
Performance Level	Poor	Wow! I kick butt!
How did I feel today?	*1 2 3 4 5 6 7 8 9 10*	
Competition Eval.	Little	A lot!
Concentration Level:	*1 2 3 4 5 6 7 8 9 10*	
Intensity Level:	*1 2 3 4 5 6 7 8 9 10*	
Relaxation Level:	*1 2 3 4 5 6 7 8 9 10*	
General Fulfillment:	*1 2 3 4 5 6 7 8 9 10*	
	Poor	Excellent
Bladework skills:	*1 2 3 4 5 6 7 8 9 10*	
Footwork skills:	*1 2 3 4 5 6 7 8 9 10*	

Great Job! Believe in yourself! Keep Working!

10 Things I need to work on:
1.
2.
3.
4.
5.
6.
7.
8.
9.
10.

10 Solutions to those things:
1.
2.
3.
4.
5.
6.
7.
8.
9.
10.

TOURNAMENT EVALUATION (PAGE 2)

10 Things I did well:
1.
2.
3.
4.
5.
6.
7.
8.
9.
10.

Need to ask my coach:
1.
2.
3.
4.
5.
6.
7.
8.
9.
10.

Do I need to change my current training plan? How?

"The will to win means nothing without the will to prepare."
~Juma Ikangaa, NYC Marathon winner

POOL SCORESHEET

Tournament: **Date:**

Name	1	2	3	4	5	6	7	V	TS	TR	Ind
1											
2											
3											
4											
5											
6											
7											

Referees:

QUICK SCOUTING OF MY POOL

Name:	Righty/Lefty	Name:	Righty/Lefty
Favorite Attack:		Favorite Attack:	
Favorite Defense:		Favorite Defense:	
Actions I think will work:		Actions I think will work:	
Name:	Righty/Lefty	Name:	Righty/Lefty
Favorite Attack:		Favorite Attack:	
Favorite Defense:		Favorite Defense:	
Actions I think will work:		Actions I think will work:	
Name:	Righty/Lefty	Name:	Righty/Lefty
Favorite Attack:		Favorite Attack:	
Favorite Defense:		Favorite Defense:	
Actions I think will work:		Actions I think will work:	
Top 3 touches from pool:		Notes about this pool:	

DIRECT ELIMINATION SCORESHEET

Direct Elimination	Tournament:																													Date:	
Table of:	yellow card								red card										black card										video ☐	V/D	
																														score	
Name/Club	1	2	3	4	5	6	7	8	9	1 0	1 1	1 2	1 3	1 4	1 5	1 6	1 7	1 8	1 9	2 0	2 1	2 2	2 3	2 4	2 5	2 6	2 7	2 8	2 9		
seed																															
	yellow card								red card										black card										video ☐		

Referee:

Actions that worked:

Actions that did not:

Actions to try next time:

Notes:

DIRECT ELIMINATION SCORESHEET

Direct Elimination	Tournament:																				Date:	
Table of:	yellow card								red card				black card								video ☐	V/D
Name/Club	1	2	3	4	5	6	7	8	9	10	11	12	13	14	15	16	17	18	19	20	21	score
seed																						
	yellow card								red card				black card								video ☐	

Referee:

Actions that worked:

Actions that did not:

Actions to try next time:

Notes:

DIRECT ELIMINATION SCORESHEET

Direct Elimination	Tournament:																									Date:	
Table of:	yellow card									red card										black card						video ☐	V/D
Name/Club	1	2	3	4	5	6	7	8	9	10	11	12	13	14	15	16	17	18	19	20	21	22	23	24	25	26	score
seed	yellow card									red card										black card						video ☐	

Referee:

Actions that worked:

Actions that did not:

Actions to try next time:

Notes:

DIRECT ELIMINATION SCORESHEET

Direct Elimination	Tournament:																												Date:	
Table of:	yellow card								red card										black card										video ☐	V/D
Name/Club	1	2	3	4	5	6	7	8	9	10	11	12	13	14	15	16	17	18	19	20	21	22	23	24	25	26	27	28	29	score
seed																														
	yellow card								red card										black card										video ☐	

Referee: _____

Actions that worked: _____

Actions that did not: _____

Actions to try next time: _____

Notes: _____

DIRECT ELIMINATION SCORESHEET

Direct Elimination	Tournament:																												Date:	
Table of:	yellow card									red card										black card								video ☐	V/D	
Name/Club	1	2	3	4	5	6	7	8	9	1 0	1 1	1 2	1 3	1 4	1 5	1 6	1 7	1 8	1 9	2 0	2 1	2 2	2 3	2 4	2 5	2 6	2 7	2 8	2 9	score
seed																														
	yellow card									red card										black card								video ☐		

Referee:

Actions that worked:

Actions that did not:

Actions to try next time:

Notes:

DIRECT ELIMINATION SCORESHEET

Direct Elimination	Tournament:																													Date:	
Table of:	yellow card									red card										black card										video ☐	V/D
																															score
Name/Club	1	2	3	4	5	6	7	8	9	1 0	1 1	1 2	1 3	1 4	1 5	1 6	1 7	1 8	1 9	2 0	2 1	2 2	2 3	2 4	2 5	2 6	2 7	2 8	2 9		
seed																															
	yellow card									red card										black card										video ☐	

Referee:

Actions that worked:

Actions that did not:

Actions to try next time:

Notes:

TOURNAMENT EVALUATION

Tournament:	Date:

Energy Level	Fatigued	Full of energy
How did I feel today?	*1 2 3 4 5 6 7 8 9 10*	
Performance Level	Poor	Wow! I kick butt!
How did I feel today?	*1 2 3 4 5 6 7 8 9 10*	
Competition Eval.	Little	A lot!
Concentration Level:	*1 2 3 4 5 6 7 8 9 10*	
Intensity Level:	*1 2 3 4 5 6 7 8 9 10*	
Relaxation Level:	*1 2 3 4 5 6 7 8 9 10*	
General Fulfillment:	*1 2 3 4 5 6 7 8 9 10*	
	Poor	Excellent
Bladework skills:	*1 2 3 4 5 6 7 8 9 10*	
Footwork skills:	*1 2 3 4 5 6 7 8 9 10*	

Great Job! Believe in yourself! Keep Working!

10 Things I need to work on:
1.
2.
3.
4.
5.
6.
7.
8.
9.
10.

10 Solutions to those things:
1.
2.
3.
4.
5.
6.
7.
8.
9.
10.

TOURNAMENT EVALUATION (PAGE 2)

10 Things I did well:
1.
2.
3.
4.
5.
6.
7.
8.
9.
10.

Need to ask my coach:
1.
2.
3.
4.
5.
6.
7.
8.
9.
10.

Do I need to change my current training plan? How?

"The will to win means nothing without the will to prepare."
~Juma Ikangaa, NYC Marathon winner

POOL SCORESHEET

Tournament: **Date:**

Name	1	2	3	4	5	6	7	V	TS	TR	Ind
1											
2											
3											
4											
5											
6											
7											

Referees:

QUICK SCOUTING OF MY POOL

Name:	Righty/Lefty	Name:	Righty/Lefty
Favorite Attack:		Favorite Attack:	
Favorite Defense:		Favorite Defense:	
Actions I think will work:		Actions I think will work:	
Name:	Righty/Lefty	Name:	Righty/Lefty
Favorite Attack:		Favorite Attack:	
Favorite Defense:		Favorite Defense:	
Actions I think will work:		Actions I think will work:	
Name:	Righty/Lefty	Name:	Righty/Lefty
Favorite Attack:		Favorite Attack:	
Favorite Defense:		Favorite Defense:	
Actions I think will work:		Actions I think will work:	
Top 3 touches from pool:		Notes about this pool:	

DIRECT ELIMINATION SCORESHEET

Direct Elimination	Tournament:																						Date:		
Table of:	yellow card									red card										black card				video ☐	
Name/Club	1	2	3	4	5	6	7	8	9	10	11	12	13	14	15	16	17	18	19	20	21	22	23	24	25	26	27	28	29	V/D
																														score
seed																														

	yellow card	red card	black card	video ☐

Referee:

Actions that worked:

Actions that did not:

Actions to try next time:

Notes:

DIRECT ELIMINATION SCORESHEET

Direct Elimination	Tournament:																													Date:	
Table of:	yellow card									red card										black card										video ☐	V/D
Name/Club	1	2	3	4	5	6	7	8	9	10	11	12	13	14	15	16	17	18	19	20	21	22	23	24	25	26	27	28	29		score
seed																															

	yellow card	red card	black card	video ☐

Referee:

Actions that worked:

Actions that did not:

Actions to try next time:

Notes:

DIRECT ELIMINATION SCORESHEET

Direct Elimination	Tournament:																													Date:	
Table of:	yellow card									red card										black card										video ☐	V/D
	1	2	3	4	5	6	7	8	9	10	11	12	13	14	15	16	17	18	19	20	21	22	23	24	25	26	27	28	29		score
Name/ Club																															
seed																															
	yellow card									red card										black card										video ☐	

Referee:

Actions that worked:

Actions that did not:

Actions to try next time:

Notes:

DIRECT ELIMINATION SCORESHEET

Direct Elimination	Tournament:																													Date:	
Table of:	yellow card									red card										black card										video ☐	V/D
Name/Club	1	2	3	4	5	6	7	8	9	10	11	12	13	14	15	16	17	18	19	20	21	22	23	24	25	26	27	28	29		score
seed																															
	yellow card									red card										black card										video ☐	

Referee:

Actions that worked:

Actions that did not:

Actions to try next time:

Notes:

DIRECT ELIMINATION SCORESHEET

Direct Elimination	Tournament:																												Date:	
Table of:	yellow card							red card									black card										video ☐			V/D
																														score
Name/ Club	1	2	3	4	5	6	7	8	9	1 0	1 1	1 2	1 3	1 4	1 5	1 6	1 7	1 8	1 9	2 0	2 1	2 2	2 3	2 4	2 5	2 6	2 7	2 8	2 9	
seed																														
	yellow card							red card									black card										video ☐			

Referee:

Actions that worked:

Actions that did not:

Actions to try next time:

Notes:

DIRECT ELIMINATION SCORESHEET

Direct Elimination	Tournament:																												Date:		
Table of:	yellow card									red card										black card									video ☐	V/D	
Name/ Club	1	2	3	4	5	6	7	8	9	10	11	12	13	14	15	16	17	18	19	20	21	22	23	24	25	26	27	28	29	score	
seed																															

yellow card red card black card video ☐

Referee:

Actions that worked:

Actions that did not:

Actions to try next time:

Notes:

TOURNAMENT EVALUATION

Tournament: **Date:**

Energy Level	Fatigued Full of energy	
How did I feel today?	1 2 3 4 5 6 7 8 9 10	
Performance Level	Poor Wow! I kick butt!	*Great Job! Believe in yourself!*
How did I feel today?	1 2 3 4 5 6 7 8 9 10	*Keep Working!*
Competition Eval.	Little A lot!	
Concentration Level:	1 2 3 4 5 6 7 8 9 10	
Intensity Level:	1 2 3 4 5 6 7 8 9 10	
Relaxation Level:	1 2 3 4 5 6 7 8 9 10	
General Fulfillment:	1 2 3 4 5 6 7 8 9 10	
	Poor Excellent	
Bladework skills:	1 2 3 4 5 6 7 8 9 10	
Footwork skills:	1 2 3 4 5 6 7 8 9 10	

10 Things I need to work on:
1.
2.
3.
4.
5.
6.
7.
8.
9.
10.

10 Solutions to those things:
1.
2.
3.
4.
5.
6.
7.
8.
9.
10.

TOURNAMENT EVALUATION (PAGE 2)

10 Things I did well:
1.
2.
3.
4.
5.
6.
7.
8.
9.
10.

Need to ask my coach:
1.
2.
3.
4.
5.
6.
7.
8.
9.
10.

Do I need to change my current training plan? How?

"The will to win means nothing without the will to prepare."
~Juma Ikangaa, NYC Marathon winner

POOL SCORESHEET

Tournament: **Date:**

Name	1	2	3	4	5	6	7	V	TS	TR	Ind
1											
2											
3											
4											
5											
6											
7											

Referees:

QUICK SCOUTING OF MY POOL

Name:	Righty/Lefty	Name:	Righty/Lefty
Favorite Attack:		Favorite Attack:	
Favorite Defense:		Favorite Defense:	
Actions I think will work:		Actions I think will work:	
Name:	Righty/Lefty	Name:	Righty/Lefty
Favorite Attack:		Favorite Attack:	
Favorite Defense:		Favorite Defense:	
Actions I think will work:		Actions I think will work:	
Name:	Righty/Lefty	Name:	Righty/Lefty
Favorite Attack:		Favorite Attack:	
Favorite Defense:		Favorite Defense:	
Actions I think will work:		Actions I think will work:	
Top 3 touches from pool:		Notes about this pool:	

DIRECT ELIMINATION SCORESHEET

Direct Elimination	Tournament:																							Date:	
Table of:	yellow card									red card										black card			video ☐	V/D	
																								score	
Name/Club	1	2	3	4	5	6	7	8	9	10	11	12	13	14	15	16	17	18	19	20	21	22	23	24	25	26	27	28	29
seed																									

	yellow card	red card	black card	video ☐

Referee:

Actions that worked:

Actions that did not:

Actions to try next time:

Notes:

DIRECT ELIMINATION SCORESHEET

Direct Elimination	Tournament:																												Date:	
Table of:	yellow card									red card										black card									video ☐	V/D
																														score
Name/Club	1	2	3	4	5	6	7	8	9	10	11	12	13	14	15	16	17	18	19	20	21	22	23	24	25	26	27	28	29	
seed																														
	yellow card									red card										black card									video ☐	

Referee:

Actions that worked:

Actions that did not:

Actions to try next time:

Notes:

DIRECT ELIMINATION SCORESHEET

Direct Elimination	Tournament:																								Date:	
Table of:	yellow card									red card										black card					video ☐	V/D
	1	2	3	4	5	6	7	8	9	10	11	12	13	14	15	16	17	18	19	20	21	22	23	24	25	score
Name/ Club																										
	yellow card									red card										black card					video ☐	
seed																										

Referee:

Actions that worked:

Actions that did not:

Actions to try next time:

Notes:

DIRECT ELIMINATION SCORESHEET

Direct Elimination	Tournament:																														Date:	
Table of:	yellow card									red card										black card										video ☐	V/D
Name/Club	1	2	3	4	5	6	7	8	9	10	11	12	13	14	15	16	17	18	19	20	21	22	23	24	25	26	27	28	29		score
seed																																
	yellow card									red card										black card										video ☐	

Referee:

Actions that worked:

Actions that did not:

Actions to try next time:

Notes:

DIRECT ELIMINATION SCORESHEET

Direct Elimination	Tournament:																													Date:	
Table of:	yellow card									red card										black card										video ☐	V/D
	1	2	3	4	5	6	7	8	9	10	11	12	13	14	15	16	17	18	19	20	21	22	23	24	25	26	27	28	29		score
Name/ Club																															
seed																															
	yellow card									red card										black card										video ☐	

Referee:

Actions that worked:

Actions that did not:

Actions to try next time:

Notes:

DIRECT ELIMINATION SCORESHEET

Direct Elimination	Tournament:																				Date:	
Table of:	yellow card									red card									black card		video ☐	V/D
	1	2	3	4	5	6	7	8	9	10	11	12	13	14	15	16	17	18	19	20		score
Name/Club																						
seed																						

yellow card	red card	black card	video ☐

Referee:

Actions that worked:

Actions that did not:

Actions to try next time:

Notes:

TOURNAMENT EVALUATION

Tournament: **Date:**

Energy Level	Fatigued Full of energy
How did I feel today?	1 2 3 4 5 6 7 8 9 10
Performance Level	Poor Wow! I kick butt!
How did I feel today?	1 2 3 4 5 6 7 8 9 10
Competition Eval.	Little A lot!
Concentration Level:	1 2 3 4 5 6 7 8 9 10
Intensity Level:	1 2 3 4 5 6 7 8 9 10
Relaxation Level:	1 2 3 4 5 6 7 8 9 10
General Fulfillment:	1 2 3 4 5 6 7 8 9 10
	Poor Excellent
Bladework skills:	1 2 3 4 5 6 7 8 9 10
Footwork skills:	1 2 3 4 5 6 7 8 9 10

Great Job! Believe in yourself! Keep Working!

10 Things I need to work on:

1.
2.
3.
4.
5.
6.
7.
8.
9.
10.

10 Solutions to those things:

1.
2.
3.
4.
5.
6.
7.
8.
9.
10.

TOURNAMENT EVALUATION (PAGE 2)

10 Things I did well:
1.
2.
3.
4.
5.
6.
7.
8.
9.
10.

Need to ask my coach:
1.
2.
3.
4.
5.
6.
7.
8.
9.
10.

Do I need to change my current training plan? How?

"The will to win means nothing without the will to prepare."
~Juma Ikangaa, NYC Marathon winner

POOL SCORESHEET

Tournament: | **Date:**

Name	1	2	3	4	5	6	7	V	TS	TR	Ind
1											
2											
3											
4											
5											
6											
7											

Referees:

QUICK SCOUTING OF MY POOL

Name:	Righty/Lefty	Name:	Righty/Lefty
Favorite Attack:		Favorite Attack:	
Favorite Defense:		Favorite Defense:	
Actions I think will work:		Actions I think will work:	
Name:	Righty/Lefty	Name:	Righty/Lefty
Favorite Attack:		Favorite Attack:	
Favorite Defense:		Favorite Defense:	
Actions I think will work:		Actions I think will work:	
Name:	Righty/Lefty	Name:	Righty/Lefty
Favorite Attack:		Favorite Attack:	
Favorite Defense:		Favorite Defense:	
Actions I think will work:		Actions I think will work:	
Top 3 touches from pool:		Notes about this pool:	

DIRECT ELIMINATION SCORESHEET

Direct Elimination	Tournament:																										Date:	
Table of:	yellow card								red card										black card								video ☐	☐
Name/ Club	1	2	3	4	5	6	7	8	9	1 0	1 1	1 2	1 3	1 4	1 5	1 6	1 7	1 8	1 9	2 0	2 1	2 2	2 3	2 4	2 5	2 6	2 7	2 8	2 9	V/D
																														score
seed																														

	yellow card	red card	black card	video ☐

Referee:

Actions that worked:

Actions that did not:

Actions to try next time:

Notes:

DIRECT ELIMINATION SCORESHEET

Direct Elimination	Tournament:																				Date:		
Table of:	yellow card									red card					black card							video ☐	V/D
																							score
Name/ Club	1	2	3	4	5	6	7	8	9	10	11	12	13	14	15	16	17	18	19	20	21	22	
seed																							
	yellow card									red card					black card							video ☐	

Referee:

Actions that worked:

Actions that did not:

Actions to try next time:

Notes:

DIRECT ELIMINATION SCORESHEET

Direct Elimination	Tournament:																											Date:		
Table of:	yellow card									red card										black card								video ☐		V/D
Name/Club	1	2	3	4	5	6	7	8	9	10	11	12	13	14	15	16	17	18	19	20	21	22	23	24	25	26	27	28	29	score
seed																															
	yellow card									red card										black card								video ☐		

Referee:

Actions that worked:

Actions that did not:

Actions to try next time:

Notes:

DIRECT ELIMINATION SCORESHEET

Direct Elimination	Tournament:																				Date:		
Table of:	yellow card									red card									black card			video ☐	V/D
Name/Club	1	2	3	4	5	6	7	8	9	10	11	12	13	14	15	16	17	18	19	20	21		score
seed																							
	yellow card									red card									black card			video ☐	

Referee:

Actions that worked:

Actions that did not:

Actions to try next time:

Notes:

DIRECT ELIMINATION SCORESHEET

Direct Elimination	Tournament:																														Date:	
Table of:	yellow card							red card										black card										video ☐			V/D	
																															score	
Name/Club	1	2	3	4	5	6	7	8	9	10	11	12	13	14	15	16	17	18	19	20	21	22	23	24	25	26	27	28	29	☐		
seed																																
	yellow card							red card										black card										video ☐				

Referee:

Actions that worked:

Actions that did not:

Actions to try next time:

Notes:

DIRECT ELIMINATION SCORESHEET

Direct Elimination	Tournament:																												Date:	
Table of:	yellow card									red card										black card									video ☐	V/D
	1	2	3	4	5	6	7	8	9	10	11	12	13	14	15	16	17	18	19	20	21	22	23	24	25	26	27	28	29	score
Name/Club																														
seed																														

yellow card red card black card video ☐

Referee:

Actions that worked:

Actions that did not:

Actions to try next time:

Notes:

TOURNAMENT EVALUATION

Tournament: **Date:**

Energy Level	Fatigued	Full of energy
How did I feel today?	*1 2 3 4 5 6 7 8 9 10*	
Performance Level	Poor	Wow! I kick butt!
How did I feel today?	*1 2 3 4 5 6 7 8 9 10*	
Competition Eval.	Little	A lot!
Concentration Level:	*1 2 3 4 5 6 7 8 9 10*	
Intensity Level:	*1 2 3 4 5 6 7 8 9 10*	
Relaxation Level:	*1 2 3 4 5 6 7 8 9 10*	
General Fulfillment:	*1 2 3 4 5 6 7 8 9 10*	
	Poor	Excellent
Bladework skills:	*1 2 3 4 5 6 7 8 9 10*	
Footwork skills:	*1 2 3 4 5 6 7 8 9 10*	

Great Job! Believe in yourself! Keep Working!

10 Things I need to work on:

1.
2.
3.
4.
5.
6.
7.
8.
9.
10.

10 Solutions to those things:

1.
2.
3.
4.
5.
6.
7.
8.
9.
10.

TOURNAMENT EVALUATION (PAGE 2)

10 Things I did well:
1.
2.
3.
4.
5.
6.
7.
8.
9.
10.

Need to ask my coach:
1.
2.
3.
4.
5.
6.
7.
8.
9.
10.

Do I need to change my current training plan? How?

"The will to win means nothing without the will to prepare."
~Juma Ikangaa, NYC Marathon winner

POOL SCORESHEET

Tournament: **Date:**

Name	1	2	3	4	5	6	7	V	TS	TR	Ind
1											
2											
3											
4											
5											
6											
7											

Referees:

QUICK SCOUTING OF MY POOL

Name:	Righty/Lefty	Name:	Righty/Lefty
Favorite Attack:		Favorite Attack:	
Favorite Defense:		Favorite Defense:	
Actions I think will work:		Actions I think will work:	
Name:	Righty/Lefty	Name:	Righty/Lefty
Favorite Attack:		Favorite Attack:	
Favorite Defense:		Favorite Defense:	
Actions I think will work:		Actions I think will work:	
Name:	Righty/Lefty	Name:	Righty/Lefty
Favorite Attack:		Favorite Attack:	
Favorite Defense:		Favorite Defense:	
Actions I think will work:		Actions I think will work:	
Top 3 touches from pool:		Notes about this pool:	

DIRECT ELIMINATION SCORESHEET

Direct Elimination	Tournament:																												Date:	
Table of:	yellow card									red card										black card									video ☐	V/D
	1	2	3	4	5	6	7	8	9	10	11	12	13	14	15	16	17	18	19	20	21	22	23	24	25	26	27	28	29	score
Name/Club																														
seed																														

	yellow card	red card	black card	video ☐
Referee:				

Actions that worked:

Actions that did not:

Actions to try next time:

Notes:

DIRECT ELIMINATION SCORESHEET

Direct Elimination	Tournament:																											Date:	
Table of:	yellow card									red card					black card									video ☐				V/D	
																												score	
Name/Club	1	2	3	4	5	6	7	8	9	1 0	1 1	1 2	1 3	1 4	1 5	1 6	1 7	1 8	1 9	2 0	2 1	2 2	2 3	2 4	2 5	2 6	2 7	2 8	2 9
seed																													

yellow card   red card   black card   video ☐

Referee:

Actions that worked:

Actions that did not:

Actions to try next time:

Notes:

DIRECT ELIMINATION SCORESHEET

Direct Elimination	Tournament:																													Date:	
Table of:	yellow card									red card										black card										video ☐	
Name/ Club	1	2	3	4	5	6	7	8	9	1 0	1 1	1 2	1 3	1 4	1 5	1 6	1 7	1 8	1 9	2 0	2 1	2 2	2 3	2 4	2 5	2 6	2 7	2 8	2 9	V/D	
																														score	
seed																															
	yellow card									red card										black card										video ☐	

Referee:

Actions that worked:

Actions that did not:

Actions to try next time:

Notes:

DIRECT ELIMINATION SCORESHEET

Direct Elimination	Tournament:																						Date:		
Table of:	yellow card									red card					black card								video ☐	V/D	
Name/ Club	1	2	3	4	5	6	7	8	9	10	11	12	13	14	15	16	17	18	19	20	21	22	23	24	score
seed																									
	yellow card									red card					black card								video ☐		

Referee:

Actions that worked:

Actions that did not:

Actions to try next time:

Notes:

DIRECT ELIMINATION SCORESHEET

Direct Elimination	Tournament:																													Date:	
Table of:	yellow card									red card										black card										video ☐	V/D
Name/Club	1	2	3	4	5	6	7	8	9	10	11	12	13	14	15	16	17	18	19	20	21	22	23	24	25	26	27	28	29		score
	yellow card									red card										black card										video ☐	
seed																															

Referee:

Actions that worked:

Actions that did not:

Actions to try next time:

Notes:

DIRECT ELIMINATION SCORESHEET

Direct Elimination	Tournament:																											Date:		
Table of:	yellow card									red card						black card										video ☐		score	V/D
Name/Club	1	2	3	4	5	6	7	8	9	10	11	12	13	14	15	16	17	18	19	20	21	22	23	24	25	26	27	28	29	
seed																														

yellow card   red card   black card   video ☐

Referee:

Actions that worked:

Actions that did not:

Actions to try next time:

Notes:

TOURNAMENT EVALUATION

Tournament: **Date:**

Energy Level	Fatigued	Full of energy
How did I feel today?	*1 2 3 4 5 6 7 8 9 10*	
Performance Level	Poor	Wow! I kick butt!
How did I feel today?	*1 2 3 4 5 6 7 8 9 10*	
Competition Eval.	Little	A lot!
Concentration Level:	*1 2 3 4 5 6 7 8 9 10*	
Intensity Level:	*1 2 3 4 5 6 7 8 9 10*	
Relaxation Level:	*1 2 3 4 5 6 7 8 9 10*	
General Fulfillment:	*1 2 3 4 5 6 7 8 9 10*	
	Poor	Excellent
Bladework skills:	*1 2 3 4 5 6 7 8 9 10*	
Footwork skills:	*1 2 3 4 5 6 7 8 9 10*	

Great Job! Believe in yourself! Keep Working!

10 Things I need to work on:
1.
2.
3.
4.
5.
6.
7.
8.
9.
10.

10 Solutions to those things:
1.
2.
3.
4.
5.
6.
7.
8.
9.
10.

TOURNAMENT EVALUATION (PAGE 2)

10 Things I did well:
1.
2.
3.
4.
5.
6.
7.
8.
9.
10.

Need to ask my coach:
1.
2.
3.
4.
5.
6.
7.
8.
9.
10.

Do I need to change my current training plan? How?

"The will to win means nothing without the will to prepare."
~Juma Ikangaa, NYC Marathon winner

POOL SCORESHEET

Tournament: **Date:**

Name	1	2	3	4	5	6	7	V	TS	TR	Ind
1											
2											
3											
4											
5											
6											
7											

Referees:

QUICK SCOUTING OF MY POOL

Name:	Righty/Lefty	Name:	Righty/Lefty
Favorite Attack:		Favorite Attack:	
Favorite Defense:		Favorite Defense:	
Actions I think will work:		Actions I think will work:	
Name:	Righty/Lefty	Name:	Righty/Lefty
Favorite Attack:		Favorite Attack:	
Favorite Defense:		Favorite Defense:	
Actions I think will work:		Actions I think will work:	
Name:	Righty/Lefty	Name:	Righty/Lefty
Favorite Attack:		Favorite Attack:	
Favorite Defense:		Favorite Defense:	
Actions I think will work:		Actions I think will work:	
Top 3 touches from pool:		Notes about this pool:	

DIRECT ELIMINATION SCORESHEET

Direct Elimination	Tournament:																												Date:	
Table of:	yellow card									red card										black card									video ☐	
	1	2	3	4	5	6	7	8	9	10	11	12	13	14	15	16	17	18	19	20	21	22	23	24	25	26	27	28	29	V/D
Name/ Club																														score
seed																														

	yellow card	red card	black card	video ☐

Referee:

Actions that worked:

Actions that did not:

Actions to try next time:

Notes:

DIRECT ELIMINATION SCORESHEET

Direct Elimination	Tournament:																													Date:	
Table of:	yellow card									red card										black card										video ☐	V/D
	1	2	3	4	5	6	7	8	9	10	11	12	13	14	15	16	17	18	19	20	21	22	23	24	25	26	27	28	29		score
Name/ Club																															
seed																															

	yellow card	red card	black card	video ☐

Referee:

Actions that worked:

Actions that did not:

Actions to try next time:

Notes:

DIRECT ELIMINATION SCORESHEET

Direct Elimination	Tournament:																													Date:	
Table of:	yellow card									red card										black card										video ☐	V/D
	1	2	3	4	5	6	7	8	9	10	11	12	13	14	15	16	17	18	19	20	21	22	23	24	25	26	27	28	29		score
Name/ Club																															
seed																															

	yellow card	red card	black card	video ☐
Referee:				

Actions that worked:

Actions that did not:

Actions to try next time:

Notes:

DIRECT ELIMINATION SCORESHEET

Direct Elimination	Tournament:																			Date:	
Table of:	yellow card									red card									black card	video ☐	
	1	2	3	4	5	6	7	8	9	10	11	12	13	14	15	16	17	18	19 20 21 22 23 24 25 26 27 28 29	V/D	
Name/Club																				score	
seed																					

	yellow card	red card	black card	video ☐

Referee:

Actions that worked:

Actions that did not:

Actions to try next time:

Notes:

DIRECT ELIMINATION SCORESHEET

Direct Elimination	Tournament:																													Date:	
Table of:	yellow card									red card									black card										video ☐	V/D	
	1	2	3	4	5	6	7	8	9	10	11	12	13	14	15	16	17	18	19	10	11	12	13	14	15	16	17	18	19	score	
Name/ Club																															
	yellow card									red card									black card										video ☐		
seed																															

Referee:

Actions that worked:

Actions that did not:

Actions to try next time:

Notes:

DIRECT ELIMINATION SCORESHEET

Direct Elimination	Tournament:																												Date:		
Table of:		yellow card								red card										black card									video ☐	V/D	
																														score	
Name/Club		1	2	3	4	5	6	7	8	9	10	11	12	13	14	15	16	17	18	19	20	21	22	23	24	25	26	27	28	29	
seed																																

	yellow card	red card	black card	video ☐

Referee:

Actions that worked:

Actions that did not:

Actions to try next time:

Notes:

TOURNAMENT EVALUATION

Tournament:	Date:

Energy Level	Fatigued	Full of energy
How did I feel today?	*1 2 3 4 5 6 7 8 9 10*	
Performance Level	Poor	Wow! I kick butt!
How did I feel today?	*1 2 3 4 5 6 7 8 9 10*	
Competition Eval.	Little	A lot!
Concentration Level:	*1 2 3 4 5 6 7 8 9 10*	
Intensity Level:	*1 2 3 4 5 6 7 8 9 10*	
Relaxation Level:	*1 2 3 4 5 6 7 8 9 10*	
General Fulfillment:	*1 2 3 4 5 6 7 8 9 10*	
	Poor	Excellent
Bladework skills:	*1 2 3 4 5 6 7 8 9 10*	
Footwork skills:	*1 2 3 4 5 6 7 8 9 10*	

Great Job! Believe in yourself! Keep Working!

10 Things I need to work on:

1.
2.
3.
4.
5.
6.
7.
8.
9.
10.

10 Solutions to those things:

1.
2.
3.
4.
5.
6.
7.
8.
9.
10.

TOURNAMENT EVALUATION (PAGE 2)

10 Things I did well:
1.
2.
3.
4.
5.
6.
7.
8.
9.
10.

Need to ask my coach:
1.
2.
3.
4.
5.
6.
7.
8.
9.
10.

Do I need to change my current training plan? How?

"The will to win means nothing without the will to prepare."
~Juma Ikangaa, NYC Marathon winner

POOL SCORESHEET

Tournament: **Date:**

Name	1	2	3	4	5	6	7	V	TS	TR	Ind
1	▓										
2		▓									
3			▓								
4				▓							
5					▓						
6						▓					
7							▓				

Referees:

QUICK SCOUTING OF MY POOL

Name:	Righty/Lefty	Name:	Righty/Lefty
Favorite Attack:		Favorite Attack:	
Favorite Defense:		Favorite Defense:	
Actions I think will work:		Actions I think will work:	
Name:	Righty/Lefty	Name:	Righty/Lefty
Favorite Attack:		Favorite Attack:	
Favorite Defense:		Favorite Defense:	
Actions I think will work:		Actions I think will work:	
Name:	Righty/Lefty	Name:	Righty/Lefty
Favorite Attack:		Favorite Attack:	
Favorite Defense:		Favorite Defense:	
Actions I think will work:		Actions I think will work:	
Top 3 touches from pool:		Notes about this pool:	

DIRECT ELIMINATION SCORESHEET

Direct Elimination	Tournament:																							Date:	
Table of:	yellow card									red card					black card					video ☐				V/D	
	1	2	3	4	5	6	7	8	9	10	11	12	13	14	15	16	17	18	19	20	21	22	23	24	25	26	27	28	29	score
Name/Club																									
seed																									

| | yellow card | | | | | | | | | red card | | | | | black card | | | | | video ☐ | |

Referee:

Actions that worked:

Actions that did not:

Actions to try next time:

Notes:

DIRECT ELIMINATION SCORESHEET

Direct Elimination	Tournament:																													Date:	
Table of:	yellow card							red card									black card										video ☐			V/D	
	1	2	3	4	5	6	7	8	9	10	11	12	13	14	15	16	17	18	19	20	21	22	23	24	25	26	27	28	29	score	
Name/Club																															
seed																															

	yellow card	red card	black card	video ☐

Referee:

Actions that worked:

Actions that did not:

Actions to try next time:

Notes:

DIRECT ELIMINATION SCORESHEET

Direct Elimination	Tournament:																				Date:	
Table of:	yellow card									red card				black card							video ☐	
Name/Club	1	2	3	4	5	6	7	8	9	10	11	12	13	14	15	16	17	18	19	20	V/D	score
seed																						
	yellow card									red card				black card							video ☐	

Referee:

Actions that worked:

Actions that did not:

Actions to try next time:

Notes:

DIRECT ELIMINATION SCORESHEET

Direct Elimination	Tournament:																										Date:	
Table of:	yellow card									red card										black card							video ☐	V/D
Name/ Club	1	2	3	4	5	6	7	8	9	10	11	12	13	14	15	16	17	18	19	20	21	22	23	24	25	26		score
seed																												

yellow card   red card   black card   video ☐

Referee:

Actions that worked:

Actions that did not:

Actions to try next time:

Notes:

DIRECT ELIMINATION SCORESHEET

Direct Elimination	Tournament:																													Date:	
Table of:	yellow card									red card										black card										video ☐	V/D
	1	2	3	4	5	6	7	8	9	10	11	12	13	14	15	16	17	18	19	20	21	22	23	24	25	26	27	28	29		score
Name/Club																															
seed																															
	yellow card									red card										black card										video ☐	

Referee:

Actions that worked:

Actions that did not:

Actions to try next time:

Notes:

TOURNAMENT EVALUATION (PAGE 2)

10 Things I did well:
1.
2.
3.
4.
5.
6.
7.
8.
9.
10.

Need to ask my coach:
1.
2.
3.
4.
5.
6.
7.
8.
9.
10.

Do I need to change my current training plan? How?

"The will to win means nothing without the will to prepare."
~Juma Ikangaa, NYC Marathon winner

POOL SCORESHEET

Tournament: **Date:**

Name	1	2	3	4	5	6	7	V	TS	TR	Ind
1	▨										
2		▨									
3			▨								
4				▨							
5					▨						
6						▨					
7							▨				

Referees:

QUICK SCOUTING OF MY POOL

Name:	Righty/Lefty	Name:	Righty/Lefty
Favorite Attack:		Favorite Attack:	
Favorite Defense:		Favorite Defense:	
Actions I think will work:		Actions I think will work:	
Name:	Righty/Lefty	Name:	Righty/Lefty
Favorite Attack:		Favorite Attack:	
Favorite Defense:		Favorite Defense:	
Actions I think will work:		Actions I think will work:	
Name:	Righty/Lefty	Name:	Righty/Lefty
Favorite Attack:		Favorite Attack:	
Favorite Defense:		Favorite Defense:	
Actions I think will work:		Actions I think will work:	
Top 3 touches from pool:		Notes about this pool:	

DIRECT ELIMINATION SCORESHEET

Direct Elimination	Tournament:																					Date:	
Table of:	yellow card									red card					black card						video ☐		V/D
																							score
Name/Club	1	2	3	4	5	6	7	8	9	10	11	12	13	14	15	16	17	18	19	20	21	22	23	24	25	26	27	28	29		
seed																								
	yellow card									red card					black card						video ☐		

Referee:

Actions that worked:

Actions that did not:

Actions to try next time:

Notes:

DIRECT ELIMINATION SCORESHEET

Direct Elimination	Tournament:																													Date:	
Table of:	yellow card									red card										black card										video ☐	V/D
Name/ Club	1	2	3	4	5	6	7	8	9	10	11	12	13	14	15	16	17	18	19	20	21	22	23	24	25	26	27	28	29		score
seed																															
	yellow card									red card										black card										video ☐	

Referee:

Actions that worked:

Actions that did not:

Actions to try next time:

Notes:

DIRECT ELIMINATION SCORESHEET

Direct Elimination	Tournament:																													Date:	
Table of:	yellow card								red card											black card									video ☐	score	V/D
	1	2	3	4	5	6	7	8	9	10	11	12	13	14	15	16	17	18	19	20	21	22	23	24	25	26	27	28	29		
Name/Club																															
	yellow card								red card											black card									video ☐		
seed																															

Referee:

Actions that worked:

Actions that did not:

Actions to try next time:

Notes:

DIRECT ELIMINATION SCORESHEET

Direct Elimination	Tournament:		Date:	
Table of:				

Name/ Club	yellow card	red card	black card	video ☐	V/D
	1 2 3 4 5 6 7 8 9	10 11 12 13 14	15 16 17 18 19	20 21 22 23 24 25 26 27 28 29	score
seed					

yellow card red card black card video ☐

Referee:

Actions that worked:

Actions that did not:

Actions to try next time:

Notes:

DIRECT ELIMINATION SCORESHEET

Direct Elimination	Tournament:																													Date:	
Table of:	yellow card									red card										black card										video ☐	V/D
	1	2	3	4	5	6	7	8	9	1 0	1 1	1 2	1 3	1 4	1 5	1 6	1 7	1 8	1 9	2 0	2 1	2 2	2 3	2 4	2 5	2 6	2 7	2 8	2 9		score
Name/Club																															
seed																															
	yellow card									red card										black card										video ☐	

Referee:

Actions that worked:

Actions that did not:

Actions to try next time:

Notes:

DIRECT ELIMINATION SCORESHEET

Direct Elimination	Tournament:																													Date:		
Table of:	yellow card									red card										black card										video ☐	V/D	
																															score	
Name/Club	1	2	3	4	5	6	7	8	9	1 0	1 1	1 2	1 3	1 4	1 5	1 6	1 7	1 8	1 9	2 0	2 1	2 2	2 3	2 4	2 5	2 6	2 7	2 8	2 9			
	yellow card									red card										black card										video ☐		
seed																																

Referee:

Actions that worked:
Actions that did not:
Actions to try next time:
Notes:

TOURNAMENT EVALUATION

Tournament:	Date:

Energy Level	Fatigued	Full of energy
How did I feel today?	*1 2 3 4 5 6 7 8 9 10*	
Performance Level	Poor	Wow! I kick butt!
How did I feel today?	*1 2 3 4 5 6 7 8 9 10*	
Competition Eval.	Little	A lot!
Concentration Level:	*1 2 3 4 5 6 7 8 9 10*	
Intensity Level:	*1 2 3 4 5 6 7 8 9 10*	
Relaxation Level:	*1 2 3 4 5 6 7 8 9 10*	
General Fulfillment:	*1 2 3 4 5 6 7 8 9 10*	
	Poor	Excellent
Bladework skills:	*1 2 3 4 5 6 7 8 9 10*	
Footwork skills:	*1 2 3 4 5 6 7 8 9 10*	

Great Job! Believe in yourself! Keep Working!

10 Things I need to work on:
1.
2.
3.
4.
5.
6.
7.
8.
9.
10.

10 Solutions to those things:
1.
2.
3.
4.
5.
6.
7.
8.
9.
10.

TOURNAMENT EVALUATION (PAGE 2)

10 Things I did well:
1.
2.
3.
4.
5.
6.
7.
8.
9.
10.

Need to ask my coach:
1.
2.
3.
4.
5.
6.
7.
8.
9.
10.

Do I need to change my current training plan? How?

"The will to win means nothing without the will to prepare."
~Juma Ikangaa, NYC Marathon winner

POOL SCORESHEET

Tournament: **Date:**

Name	1	2	3	4	5	6	7	V	TS	TR	Ind
1											
2											
3											
4											
5											
6											
7											

Referees:

QUICK SCOUTING OF MY POOL

Name:	Righty/Lefty	Name:	Righty/Lefty
Favorite Attack:		Favorite Attack:	
Favorite Defense:		Favorite Defense:	
Actions I think will work:		Actions I think will work:	
Name:	Righty/Lefty	Name:	Righty/Lefty
Favorite Attack:		Favorite Attack:	
Favorite Defense:		Favorite Defense:	
Actions I think will work:		Actions I think will work:	
Name:	Righty/Lefty	Name:	Righty/Lefty
Favorite Attack:		Favorite Attack:	
Favorite Defense:		Favorite Defense:	
Actions I think will work:		Actions I think will work:	
Top 3 touches from pool:		Notes about this pool:	

DIRECT ELIMINATION SCORESHEET

Direct Elimination	Tournament:																											Date:	
Table of:	yellow card								red card										black card									video ☐	V/D
	1	2	3	4	5	6	7	8	9	10	11	12	13	14	15	16	17	18	19	20	21	22	23	24	25	26	27	28	29	score
Name/Club																														
seed																														
	yellow card								red card										black card									video ☐	

Referee:

Actions that worked:

Actions that did not:

Actions to try next time:

Notes:

DIRECT ELIMINATION SCORESHEET

Direct Elimination	Tournament:																													Date:	
Table of:	yellow card									red card										black card										video ☐	
Name/Club	1	2	3	4	5	6	7	8	9	1/0	1/1	1/2	1/3	1/4	1/5	1/6	1/7	1/8	1/9	2/0	2/1	2/2	2/3	2/4	2/5	2/6	2/7	2/8	2/9	V/D	
																														score	
seed																															
	yellow card									red card										black card										video ☐	

Referee:

Actions that worked:

Actions that did not:

Actions to try next time:

Notes:

DIRECT ELIMINATION SCORESHEET

Direct Elimination	Tournament:																													Date:	
Table of:	yellow card									red card										black card									video ☐	V/D
																															score
Name/Club	1	2	3	4	5	6	7	8	9	10	11	12	13	14	15	16	17	18	19	20	21	22	23	24	25	26	27	28	29	
seed																															

	yellow card	red card	black card	video ☐
Referee:				

Actions that worked:

Actions that did not:

Actions to try next time:

Notes:

DIRECT ELIMINATION SCORESHEET

Direct Elimination	Tournament:																												Date:	
Table of:	yellow card									red card										black card									video ☐	V/D
Name/ Club	1	2	3	4	5	6	7	8	9	10	11	12	13	14	15	16	17	18	19	20	21	22	23	24	25	26	27	28	29	score
seed																														

yellow card   red card   black card   video ☐

Referee:

Actions that worked:

Actions that did not:

Actions to try next time:

Notes:

DIRECT ELIMINATION SCORESHEET

Direct Elimination	Tournament:																				Date:		
Table of:	yellow card								red card						black card						video ☐		
Name/Club	1	2	3	4	5	6	7	8	9	10	11	12	13	14	15	16	17	18	19	20	21	22	score
																							V/D
seed																							

	yellow card	red card	black card	video ☐

Referee:

Actions that worked:

Actions that did not:

Actions to try next time:

Notes:

DIRECT ELIMINATION SCORESHEET

Direct Elimination	Tournament:																												Date:	
Table of:	yellow card									red card										black card									video ☐	V/D
Name/ Club	1	2	3	4	5	6	7	8	9	10	11	12	13	14	15	16	17	18	19	20	21	22	23	24	25	26	27	28	29	score
seed																														

yellow card　　　red card　　　black card　　　video ☐

Referee:

Actions that worked:
Actions that did not:
Actions to try next time:
Notes:

TOURNAMENT EVALUATION

Tournament: **Date:**

Energy Level	Fatigued	Full of energy
How did I feel today?	*1 2 3 4 5 6 7 8 9 10*	
Performance Level	Poor	Wow! I kick butt!
How did I feel today?	*1 2 3 4 5 6 7 8 9 10*	
Competition Eval.	Little	A lot!
Concentration Level:	*1 2 3 4 5 6 7 8 9 10*	
Intensity Level:	*1 2 3 4 5 6 7 8 9 10*	
Relaxation Level:	*1 2 3 4 5 6 7 8 9 10*	
General Fulfillment:	*1 2 3 4 5 6 7 8 9 10*	
	Poor	Excellent
Bladework skills:	*1 2 3 4 5 6 7 8 9 10*	
Footwork skills:	*1 2 3 4 5 6 7 8 9 10*	

Great Job! Believe in yourself! Keep Working!

10 Things I need to work on:
1.
2.
3.
4.
5.
6.
7.
8.
9.
10.

10 Solutions to those things:
1.
2.
3.
4.
5.
6.
7.
8.
9.
10.

TOURNAMENT EVALUATION (PAGE 2)

10 Things I did well:
1.
2.
3.
4.
5.
6.
7.
8.
9.
10.

Need to ask my coach:
1.
2.
3.
4.
5.
6.
7.
8.
9.
10.

Do I need to change my current training plan? How?

"The will to win means nothing without the will to prepare."
~Juma Ikangaa, NYC Marathon winner

SCOUTING (SAMPLE)

Name:	Lynch, B		Country/Division:	
Club:	Forte Fencing		USA	
Age group:	Y10 Y12 Y14 CDT JNR **OPEN** VET			
Visuals:	**Righty**	Lefty	Taller	**Shorter**	Growing
Trends:	**Attacker**	Defender	Counter attacker		
Tactics:	**Tactical**	Sometimes Tactical	Not Very Tactical		
Timing:	Slow/**Quick**		Poor/**Good Timing**	
	Awkward Timing		Arrhythmic Timing	
Opponent In the Box:	Attack in Prep	**Varies target**		
Closeout	Beat attacks	**Parry-Riposte**		
Feint deceive	Counter Attack with (timing)(closeout)			
Big steps	Pull Distance (make me fall short)	Other:		
Opponent Attacks:	Simple	Composed	**Long smooth attacks**	
Big steps	Small steps	Beat attacks	Strong Blade Actions	
Search + Take Blade	Feint deceive **(lateral)** (circular)			
Counter Attack (timing)(body displacement)(opposition):				
Opponent Defense:	Parry: 2 3 4 5	Circle: 2 **3** 4		
Sweeping parries while retreating	Counter time	2 parries		
Actions that worked:	Parry riposte 2 3 4 5	Circle: 2 3 4		
Pull distance – make opp fall short	Push and attack	Pull and defend		
Feint deceive **(4-6)** (circle 3) (around 2) ( ) ( )				
Beat-disengage	**False parry-real parry riposte**			
Notes:	False parry real parry worked the best. Next time figure out how to bait her better into a panic parry			
Observed on:	2/17/17	2/17/17		
Opponent:	Me	Edwards		
Who won?	Me	Lynch		
Score	5-4	5-2		

SCOUTING PRACTICE

Name:					Country/Division:	
Club:						
Age group:	Y10	Y12	Y14	CDT	JNR	OPEN	VET
Visuals:	Righty	Lefty	Taller	Shorter	Growing
Trends:	Attacker	Defender	Counter attacker	
Tactics:	Tactical	Sometimes Tactical	Not Very Tactical
Timing:	Slow/Quick		Poor/Good Timing	
	Awkward Timing		Arrhythmic Timing	

Opponent In the Box:	Attack in Prep	Varies target
Closeout	Beat attacks	Parry-Riposte
Feint deceive	Counter Attack with (timing)(closeout)	
Big steps	Pull Distance (make me fall short)	Other:

Opponent Attacks:		Simple	Composed	Long smooth attacks
Big steps	Small steps	Beat attacks		Strong Blade Actions
Search + Take Blade	Feint deceive (lateral)(circular)			
Counter Attack (timing)(body displacement)(opposition):				

Opponent Defense:	Parry: 2 3 4 5	Circle: 2 3 4
Sweeping parries while retreating	Counter time	2 parries

Actions that worked:	Parry riposte 2 3 4 5	Circle: 2 3 4
Pull distance – make opp fall short	Push and attack	Pull and defend
Feint deceive (4-6) (circle 3) (around 2) ( ) ( )		
Beat-disengage	False parry-real parry riposte	

Notes:

Observed on:					
Opponent:					
Who won?					
Score					

SCOUTING PRACTICE

Name:		Country/Division:	
Club:			

Age group:	Y10	Y12	Y14	CDT	JNR	OPEN	VET
Visuals:	Righty	Lefty		Taller	Shorter	Growing	
Trends:	Attacker	Defender		Counter attacker			
Tactics:	Tactical	Sometimes Tactical		Not Very Tactical			
Timing:	Slow/Quick			Poor/Good Timing			
	Awkward Timing			Arrhythmic Timing			

Opponent In the Box:		Attack in Prep	Varies target	
Closeout		Beat attacks	Parry-Riposte	
Feint deceive		Counter Attack with (timing)(closeout)		
Big steps	Pull Distance (make me fall short)		Other:	

Opponent Attacks:		Simple	Composed	Long smooth attacks
Big steps	Small steps	Beat attacks		Strong Blade Actions
Search + Take Blade		Feint deceive (lateral)(circular)		
Counter Attack (timing)(body displacement)(opposition):				

Opponent Defense:	Parry: 2 3 4 5		Circle: 2 3 4	
Sweeping parries while retreating		Counter time		2 parries

Actions that worked:	Parry riposte 2 3 4 5	Circle: 2 3 4	
Pull distance – make opp fall short		Push and attack	Pull and defend
Feint deceive (4-6) (circle 3) (around 2) (	) (	)	
Beat-disengage	False parry-real parry riposte		

Notes:	

Observed on:					
Opponent:					
Who won?					
Score					

SCOUTING PRACTICE

Name:		Country/Division:	
Club:			

Age group:	Y10	Y12	Y14	CDT	JNR	OPEN	VET
Visuals:	Righty	Lefty	Taller		Shorter		Growing
Trends:	Attacker	Defender	Counter attacker				
Tactics:	Tactical	Sometimes Tactical			Not Very Tactical		

Timing:	Slow/Quick	Poor/Good Timing
	Awkward Timing	Arrhythmic Timing

Opponent In the Box:	Attack in Prep	Varies target
Closeout	Beat attacks	Parry-Riposte
Feint deceive	Counter Attack with (timing)(closeout)	
Big steps	Pull Distance (make me fall short)	Other:

Opponent Attacks:	Simple	Composed	Long smooth attacks
Big steps	Small steps	Beat attacks	Strong Blade Actions
Search + Take Blade	Feint deceive (lateral)(circular)		
Counter Attack (timing)(body displacement)(opposition):			

Opponent Defense:	Parry: 2 3 4 5	Circle: 2 3 4
Sweeping parries while retreating	Counter time	2 parries

Actions that worked:	Parry riposte 2 3 4 5	Circle: 2 3 4
Pull distance – make opp fall short	Push and attack	Pull and defend
Feint deceive (4-6) (circle 3) (around 2) ( ) ( )		
Beat-disengage	False parry-real parry riposte	

Notes:

Observed on:				
Opponent:				
Who won?				
Score				

SCOUTING PRACTICE

Name:		Country/Division:	
Club:			
Age group:	Y10 Y12 Y14 CDT	JNR OPEN VET	
Visuals:	Righty	Lefty	Taller	Shorter	Growing
Trends:	Attacker	Defender	Counter attacker	
Tactics:	Tactical	Sometimes Tactical	Not Very Tactical	
Timing:	Slow/Quick	Poor/Good Timing		
	Awkward Timing	Arrhythmic Timing		

Opponent In the Box:	Attack in Prep	Varies target
Closeout	Beat attacks	Parry-Riposte
Feint deceive	Counter Attack with (timing)(closeout)	
Big steps	Pull Distance (make me fall short)	Other:

Opponent Attacks:	Simple	Composed	Long smooth attacks
Big steps	Small steps	Beat attacks	Strong Blade Actions
Search + Take Blade	Feint deceive (lateral)(circular)		
Counter Attack (timing)(body displacement)(opposition):			

Opponent Defense:	Parry: 2 3 4 5	Circle: 2 3 4	
Sweeping parries while retreating	Counter time		2 parries

Actions that worked:	Parry riposte 2 3 4 5	Circle: 2 3 4	
Pull distance – make opp fall short		Push and attack	Pull and defend
Feint deceive (4-6) (circle 3) (around 2) (	) (	)	
Beat-disengage	False parry-real parry riposte		

Notes:

Observed on:					
Opponent:					
Who won?					
Score					

SCOUTING

Name:		Country/Division:	A
Club:			

Age group:	Y10	Y12	Y14	CDT	JNR	OPEN	VET
Visuals:	Righty	Lefty		Taller	Shorter		Growing
Trends:	Attacker	Defender		Counter attacker			
Tactics:	Tactical		Sometimes Tactical		Not Very Tactical		
Timing:	Slow/Quick			Poor/Good Timing			
	Awkward Timing			Arrhythmic Timing			

Opponent In the Box:	Attack in Prep		Varies target	
Closeout	Beat attacks		Parry-Riposte	
Feint deceive	Counter Attack with (timing)(closeout)			
Big steps	Pull Distance (make me fall short)		Other:	

Opponent Attacks:		Simple	Composed	Long smooth attacks
Big steps	Small steps	Beat attacks		Strong Blade Actions
Search + Take Blade		Feint deceive (lateral)(circular)		
Counter Attack (timing)(body displacement)(opposition):				

Opponent Defense:	Parry: 2 3 4 5		Circle: 2 3 4	
Sweeping parries while retreating		Counter time		2 parries

Actions that worked:	Parry riposte 2 3 4 5		Circle: 2 3 4
Pull distance – make opp fall short		Push and attack	Pull and defend
Feint deceive (4-6) (circle 3) (around 2) (	) (		)
Beat-disengage	False parry-real parry riposte		

Notes:	

Observed on:					
Opponent:					
Who won?					
Score					

A

Name:		Country/Division:	
Club:			
Age group:	Y10 Y12 Y14 CDT	JNR OPEN VET	
Visuals:	Righty	Lefty	Taller	Shorter	Growing
Trends:	Attacker	Defender	Counter attacker	
Tactics:	Tactical	Sometimes Tactical	Not Very Tactical	
Timing:	Slow/Quick	Poor/Good Timing	
	Awkward Timing	Arrhythmic Timing	

Opponent In the Box:	Attack in Prep	Varies target
Closeout	Beat attacks	Parry-Riposte
Feint deceive	Counter Attack with (timing)(closeout)	
Big steps	Pull Distance (make me fall short)	Other:

Opponent Attacks:	Simple	Composed	Long smooth attacks
Big steps	Small steps	Beat attacks	Strong Blade Actions
Search + Take Blade	Feint deceive (lateral)(circular)		
Counter Attack (timing)(body displacement)(opposition):			

Opponent Defense:	Parry: 2 3 4 5	Circle: 2 3 4
Sweeping parries while retreating	Counter time	2 parries

Actions that worked:	Parry riposte 2 3 4 5	Circle: 2 3 4
Pull distance – make opp fall short	Push and attack	Pull and defend
Feint deceive (4-6) (circle 3) (around 2) (	) (	)
Beat-disengage	False parry-real parry riposte	

Notes:

Observed on:				
Opponent:				
Who won?				
Score				

Name:					Country/Division:		A
Club:							
Age group:	Y10	Y12	Y14	CDT	JNR	OPEN	VET
Visuals:	Righty	Lefty	Taller		Shorter		Growing
Trends:	Attacker	Defender	Counter attacker				
Tactics:	Tactical	Sometimes Tactical			Not Very Tactical		
Timing:	Slow/Quick			Poor/Good Timing			
	Awkward Timing			Arrhythmic Timing			

Opponent In the Box:	Attack in Prep		Varies target	
Closeout	Beat attacks		Parry-Riposte	
Feint deceive	Counter Attack with (timing)(closeout)			
Big steps	Pull Distance (make me fall short)		Other:	
Opponent Attacks:	Simple	Composed	Long smooth attacks	
Big steps	Small steps	Beat attacks	Strong Blade Actions	
Search + Take Blade	Feint deceive (lateral)(circular)			
Counter Attack (timing)(body displacement)(opposition):				
Opponent Defense:	Parry: 2 3 4 5		Circle: 2 3 4	
Sweeping parries while retreating	Counter time		2 parries	
Actions that worked:	Parry riposte 2 3 4 5		Circle: 2 3 4	
Pull distance – make opp fall short		Push and attack	Pull and defend	
Feint deceive (4-6) (circle 3) (around 2) ( ) ( )				
Beat-disengage	False parry-real parry riposte			

Notes:				

Observed on:				
Opponent:				
Who won?				
Score				

A	Name:					Country/Division:		
	Club:							
	Age group:	Y10	Y12	Y14	CDT	JNR	OPEN	VET
	Visuals:	Righty	Lefty	Taller		Shorter		Growing
	Trends:	Attacker	Defender	Counter attacker				
	Tactics:	Tactical	Sometimes Tactical			Not Very Tactical		
	Timing:	Slow/Quick			Poor/Good Timing			
		Awkward Timing			Arrhythmic Timing			

Opponent In the Box:		Attack in Prep		Varies target	
Closeout		Beat attacks		Parry-Riposte	
Feint deceive		Counter Attack with (timing)(closeout)			
Big steps	Pull Distance (make me fall short)			Other:	
Opponent Attacks:		Simple	Composed	Long smooth attacks	
Big steps	Small steps	Beat attacks		Strong Blade Actions	
Search + Take Blade		Feint deceive (lateral)(circular)			
Counter Attack (timing)(body displacement)(opposition):					
Opponent Defense:		Parry: 2 3 4 5		Circle: 2 3 4	
Sweeping parries while retreating		Counter time			2 parries
Actions that worked:		Parry riposte 2 3 4 5		Circle: 2 3 4	
Pull distance – make opp fall short			Push and attack		Pull and defend
Feint deceive (4-6) (circle 3) (around 2) ( ) ( )					
Beat-disengage		False parry-real parry riposte			
Notes:					
Observed on:					
Opponent:					
Who won?					
Score					

B

Name:				Country/Division:	
Club:					
Age group:	Y10	Y12	Y14	CDT	JNR	OPEN	VET
Visuals:	Righty	Lefty	Taller	Shorter	Growing
Trends:	Attacker	Defender	Counter attacker	
Tactics:	Tactical	Sometimes Tactical	Not Very Tactical
Timing:	Slow/Quick		Poor/Good Timing	
	Awkward Timing		Arrhythmic Timing	

Opponent In the Box:	Attack in Prep	Varies target
Closeout	Beat attacks	Parry-Riposte
Feint deceive	Counter Attack with (timing)(closeout)	
Big steps	Pull Distance (make me fall short)	Other:

Opponent Attacks:		Simple	Composed	Long smooth attacks
Big steps	Small steps	Beat attacks		Strong Blade Actions
Search + Take Blade	Feint deceive (lateral)(circular)			
Counter Attack (timing)(body displacement)(opposition):				

Opponent Defense:	Parry: 2 3 4 5	Circle: 2 3 4
Sweeping parries while retreating	Counter time	2 parries

Actions that worked:	Parry riposte 2 3 4 5	Circle: 2 3 4
Pull distance – make opp fall short	Push and attack	Pull and defend
Feint deceive (4-6) (circle 3) (around 2) ( ) ( )		
Beat-disengage	False parry-real parry riposte	

Notes:

Observed on:				
Opponent:				
Who won?				
Score				

B

Name:					Country/Division:	
Club:						
Age group:	Y10	Y12	Y14	CDT	JNR OPEN	VET
Visuals:	Righty	Lefty	Taller		Shorter	Growing
Trends:	Attacker	Defender	Counter attacker			
Tactics:	Tactical	Sometimes Tactical			Not Very Tactical	
Timing:	Slow/Quick			Poor/Good Timing		
	Awkward Timing			Arrhythmic Timing		

Opponent In the Box:		Attack in Prep		Varies target	
Closeout		Beat attacks		Parry-Riposte	
Feint deceive		Counter Attack with (timing)(closeout)			
Big steps	Pull Distance (make me fall short)			Other:	
Opponent Attacks:		Simple	Composed	Long smooth attacks	
Big steps	Small steps	Beat attacks		Strong Blade Actions	
Search + Take Blade		Feint deceive (lateral)(circular)			
Counter Attack (timing)(body displacement)(opposition):					
Opponent Defense:		Parry: 2 3 4 5		Circle: 2 3 4	
Sweeping parries while retreating		Counter time		2 parries	
Actions that worked:		Parry riposte 2 3 4 5		Circle: 2 3 4	
Pull distance – make opp fall short		Push and attack		Pull and defend	
Feint deceive (4-6) (circle 3) (around 2) ( ) ( )					
Beat-disengage		False parry-real parry riposte			
Notes:					

Observed on:					
Opponent:					
Who won?					
Score					

B

Name:					Country/Division:		
Club:							
Age group:	Y10	Y12	Y14	CDT	JNR	OPEN	VET
Visuals:	Righty	Lefty	Taller		Shorter		Growing
Trends:	Attacker	Defender	Counter attacker				
Tactics:	Tactical	Sometimes Tactical			Not Very Tactical		
Timing:	Slow/Quick				Poor/Good Timing		
	Awkward Timing				Arrhythmic Timing		

Opponent In the Box:		Attack in Prep		Varies target	
Closeout		Beat attacks		Parry-Riposte	
Feint deceive		Counter Attack with (timing)(closeout)			
Big steps	Pull Distance (make me fall short)			Other:	

Opponent Attacks:		Simple	Composed	Long smooth attacks	
Big steps	Small steps	Beat attacks		Strong Blade Actions	
Search + Take Blade	Feint deceive (lateral)(circular)				
Counter Attack (timing)(body displacement)(opposition):					

Opponent Defense:		Parry: 2 3 4 5		Circle: 2 3 4	
Sweeping parries while retreating		Counter time		2 parries	

Actions that worked:		Parry riposte 2 3 4 5		Circle: 2 3 4	
Pull distance – make opp fall short			Push and attack	Pull and defend	
Feint deceive (4-6) (circle 3) (around 2) (		) (	)		
Beat-disengage		False parry-real parry riposte			

Notes:				

Observed on:					
Opponent:					
Who won?					
Score					

B

Name:		Country/Division:	
Club:			

Age group:	Y10	Y12	Y14	CDT	JNR	OPEN	VET
Visuals:	Righty	Lefty		Taller	Shorter	Growing	
Trends:	Attacker	Defender		Counter attacker			
Tactics:	Tactical	Sometimes Tactical		Not Very Tactical			
Timing:	Slow/Quick			Poor/Good Timing			
	Awkward Timing			Arrhythmic Timing			

Opponent In the Box:		Attack in Prep	Varies target	
Closeout		Beat attacks	Parry-Riposte	
Feint deceive		Counter Attack with (timing)(closeout)		
Big steps	Pull Distance (make me fall short)		Other:	
Opponent Attacks:		Simple	Composed	Long smooth attacks
Big steps	Small steps	Beat attacks		Strong Blade Actions
Search + Take Blade		Feint deceive (lateral)(circular)		
Counter Attack (timing)(body displacement)(opposition):				
Opponent Defense:		Parry: 2 3 4 5	Circle: 2 3 4	
Sweeping parries while retreating		Counter time		2 parries
Actions that worked:		Parry riposte 2 3 4 5	Circle: 2 3 4	
Pull distance – make opp fall short		Push and attack	Pull and defend	
Feint deceive (4-6) (circle 3) (around 2) (		) (	)	
Beat-disengage		False parry-real parry riposte		

Notes:	

Observed on:					
Opponent:					
Who won?					
Score					

B

Name:				Country/Division:	
Club:					
Age group:	Y10	Y12	Y14	CDT	JNR	OPEN	VET
Visuals:	Righty	Lefty	Taller	Shorter	Growing
Trends:	Attacker	Defender	Counter attacker	
Tactics:	Tactical	Sometimes Tactical	Not Very Tactical	
Timing:	Slow/Quick		Poor/Good Timing	
	Awkward Timing		Arrhythmic Timing	

Opponent In the Box:	Attack in Prep	Varies target
Closeout	Beat attacks	Parry-Riposte
Feint deceive	Counter Attack with (timing)(closeout)	
Big steps	Pull Distance (make me fall short)	Other:

Opponent Attacks:	Simple	Composed	Long smooth attacks
Big steps	Small steps	Beat attacks	Strong Blade Actions
Search + Take Blade	Feint deceive (lateral)(circular)		
Counter Attack (timing)(body displacement)(opposition):			

Opponent Defense:	Parry: 2 3 4 5	Circle: 2 3 4
Sweeping parries while retreating	Counter time	2 parries

Actions that worked:	Parry riposte 2 3 4 5	Circle: 2 3 4
Pull distance – make opp fall short	Push and attack	Pull and defend
Feint deceive (4-6) (circle 3) (around 2) ( ) ( )		
Beat-disengage	False parry-real parry riposte	

Notes:				
Observed on:				
Opponent:				
Who won?				
Score				

B

Name:		Country/Division:	
Club:			

Age group:	Y10	Y12	Y14	CDT	JNR	OPEN	VET
Visuals:	Righty	Lefty	Taller		Shorter		Growing
Trends:	Attacker	Defender	Counter attacker				
Tactics:	Tactical	Sometimes Tactical			Not Very Tactical		
Timing:	Slow/Quick			Poor/Good Timing			
	Awkward Timing			Arrhythmic Timing			

Opponent In the Box:		Attack in Prep		Varies target	
Closeout		Beat attacks		Parry-Riposte	
Feint deceive		Counter Attack with (timing)(closeout)			
Big steps	Pull Distance (make me fall short)			Other:	
Opponent Attacks:		Simple	Composed	Long smooth attacks	
Big steps	Small steps	Beat attacks		Strong Blade Actions	
Search + Take Blade		Feint deceive (lateral)(circular)			
Counter Attack (timing)(body displacement)(opposition):					
Opponent Defense:		Parry: 2 3 4 5		Circle: 2 3 4	
Sweeping parries while retreating		Counter time			2 parries
Actions that worked:		Parry riposte 2 3 4 5		Circle: 2 3 4	
Pull distance – make opp fall short			Push and attack	Pull and defend	
Feint deceive (4-6) (circle 3) (around 2) ( ) ( )					
Beat-disengage		False parry-real parry riposte			

Notes:	

Observed on:					
Opponent:					
Who won?					
Score					

B

Name:					Country/Division:	
Club:						
Age group:	Y10	Y12	Y14	CDT	JNR	OPEN	VET
Visuals:	Righty	Lefty	Taller		Shorter	Growing
Trends:	Attacker	Defender	Counter attacker			
Tactics:	Tactical	Sometimes Tactical			Not Very Tactical	
Timing:	Slow/Quick			Poor/Good Timing		
	Awkward Timing			Arrhythmic Timing		

Opponent In the Box:	Attack in Prep		Varies target	
Closeout	Beat attacks		Parry-Riposte	
Feint deceive	Counter Attack with (timing)(closeout)			
Big steps	Pull Distance (make me fall short)		Other:	

Opponent Attacks:	Simple	Composed	Long smooth attacks
Big steps	Small steps	Beat attacks	Strong Blade Actions
Search + Take Blade	Feint deceive (lateral)(circular)		
Counter Attack (timing)(body displacement)(opposition):			

Opponent Defense:	Parry: 2 3 4 5		Circle: 2 3 4
Sweeping parries while retreating	Counter time		2 parries

Actions that worked:	Parry riposte 2 3 4 5		Circle: 2 3 4
Pull distance – make opp fall short		Push and attack	Pull and defend
Feint deceive (4-6) (circle 3) (around 2) ( ) ( )			
Beat-disengage	False parry-real parry riposte		

Notes:

Observed on:					
Opponent:					
Who won?					
Score					

B

Name:		Country/Division:	
Club:			

Age group:	Y10	Y12	Y14	CDT	JNR	OPEN	VET
Visuals:	Righty	Lefty	Taller		Shorter		Growing
Trends:	Attacker	Defender	Counter attacker				
Tactics:	Tactical	Sometimes Tactical		Not Very Tactical			

Timing:	Slow/Quick	Poor/Good Timing
	Awkward Timing	Arrhythmic Timing

Opponent In the Box:	Attack in Prep	Varies target
Closeout	Beat attacks	Parry-Riposte
Feint deceive	Counter Attack with (timing)(closeout)	
Big steps	Pull Distance (make me fall short)	Other:

Opponent Attacks:	Simple	Composed	Long smooth attacks
Big steps	Small steps	Beat attacks	Strong Blade Actions
Search + Take Blade	Feint deceive (lateral)(circular)		
Counter Attack (timing)(body displacement)(opposition):			

Opponent Defense:	Parry: 2 3 4 5	Circle: 2 3 4	
Sweeping parries while retreating	Counter time		2 parries

Actions that worked:	Parry riposte 2 3 4 5	Circle: 2 3 4
Pull distance – make opp fall short	Push and attack	Pull and defend
Feint deceive (4-6) (circle 3) (around 2) ( ) ( )		
Beat-disengage	False parry-real parry riposte	

Notes:	

Observed on:					
Opponent:					
Who won?					
Score					

Name:					Country/Division:		
Club:							
Age group:	Y10	Y12	Y14	CDT	JNR	OPEN	VET
Visuals:	Righty	Lefty		Taller		Shorter	Growing
Trends:	Attacker	Defender		Counter attacker			
Tactics:	Tactical	Sometimes Tactical			Not Very Tactical		
Timing:	Slow/Quick				Poor/Good Timing		
	Awkward Timing				Arrhythmic Timing		

Opponent In the Box:	Attack in Prep		Varies target	
Closeout	Beat attacks		Parry-Riposte	
Feint deceive	Counter Attack with (timing)(closeout)			
Big steps	Pull Distance (make me fall short)			Other:

Opponent Attacks:	Simple	Composed	Long smooth attacks
Big steps	Small steps	Beat attacks	Strong Blade Actions
Search + Take Blade	Feint deceive (lateral)(circular)		
Counter Attack (timing)(body displacement)(opposition):			

Opponent Defense:	Parry: 2 3 4 5		Circle: 2 3 4	
Sweeping parries while retreating		Counter time		2 parries

Actions that worked:	Parry riposte 2 3 4 5	Circle: 2 3 4
Pull distance – make opp fall short	Push and attack	Pull and defend
Feint deceive (4-6) (circle 3) (around 2) ( ) ( )		
Beat-disengage	False parry-real parry riposte	

Notes:

Observed on:				
Opponent:				
Who won?				
Score				

C

Name:				Country/Division:	
Club:					
Age group:	Y10	Y12	Y14	CDT	JNR	OPEN	VET
Visuals:	Righty	Lefty	Taller	Shorter	Growing
Trends:	Attacker	Defender	Counter attacker		
Tactics:	Tactical	Sometimes Tactical	Not Very Tactical		
Timing:	Slow/Quick		Poor/Good Timing		
	Awkward Timing		Arrhythmic Timing		

Opponent In the Box:	Attack in Prep	Varies target
Closeout	Beat attacks	Parry-Riposte
Feint deceive	Counter Attack with (timing)(closeout)	
Big steps	Pull Distance (make me fall short)	Other:

Opponent Attacks:	Simple	Composed	Long smooth attacks
Big steps	Small steps	Beat attacks	Strong Blade Actions
Search + Take Blade	Feint deceive (lateral)(circular)		
Counter Attack (timing)(body displacement)(opposition):			

Opponent Defense:	Parry: 2 3 4 5	Circle: 2 3 4
Sweeping parries while retreating	Counter time	2 parries

Actions that worked:	Parry riposte 2 3 4 5	Circle: 2 3 4
Pull distance – make opp fall short	Push and attack	Pull and defend
Feint deceive (4-6) (circle 3) (around 2) ( ) ( )		
Beat-disengage	False parry-real parry riposte	

Notes:

Observed on:					
Opponent:					
Who won?					
Score					

Name:					Country/Division:		
Club:							
Age group:	Y10	Y12	Y14	CDT	JNR	OPEN	VET
Visuals:	Righty	Lefty	Taller		Shorter		Growing
Trends:	Attacker	Defender	Counter attacker				
Tactics:	Tactical	Sometimes Tactical			Not Very Tactical		
Timing:	Slow/Quick			Poor/Good Timing			
	Awkward Timing			Arrhythmic Timing			

Opponent In the Box:	Attack in Prep		Varies target	
Closeout		Beat attacks		Parry-Riposte
Feint deceive		Counter Attack with (timing)(closeout)		
Big steps	Pull Distance (make me fall short)			Other:

Opponent Attacks:	Simple		Composed	Long smooth attacks
Big steps	Small steps	Beat attacks		Strong Blade Actions
Search + Take Blade	Feint deceive (lateral)(circular)			
Counter Attack (timing)(body displacement)(opposition):				

Opponent Defense:	Parry: 2 3 4 5		Circle: 2 3 4	
Sweeping parries while retreating		Counter time		2 parries

Actions that worked:	Parry riposte 2 3 4 5		Circle: 2 3 4
Pull distance – make opp fall short		Push and attack	Pull and defend
Feint deceive (4-6) (circle 3) (around 2) ( ) ( )			
Beat-disengage	False parry-real parry riposte		

Notes:

Observed on:					
Opponent:					
Who won?					
Score					

C

C

Name:					Country/Division:	
Club:						
Age group:	Y10	Y12	Y14	CDT	JNR	OPEN	VET
Visuals:	Righty	Lefty	Taller		Shorter	Growing
Trends:	Attacker	Defender	Counter attacker			
Tactics:	Tactical	Sometimes Tactical		Not Very Tactical		
Timing:	Slow/Quick		Poor/Good Timing			
	Awkward Timing		Arrhythmic Timing			

Opponent In the Box:	Attack in Prep	Varies target
Closeout	Beat attacks	Parry-Riposte
Feint deceive	Counter Attack with (timing)(closeout)	
Big steps	Pull Distance (make me fall short)	Other:

Opponent Attacks:	Simple	Composed	Long smooth attacks
Big steps	Small steps	Beat attacks	Strong Blade Actions
Search + Take Blade	Feint deceive (lateral)(circular)		
Counter Attack (timing)(body displacement)(opposition):			

Opponent Defense:	Parry: 2 3 4 5	Circle: 2 3 4
Sweeping parries while retreating	Counter time	2 parries

Actions that worked:	Parry riposte 2 3 4 5	Circle: 2 3 4
Pull distance – make opp fall short	Push and attack	Pull and defend
Feint deceive (4-6) (circle 3) (around 2) ( ) ( )		
Beat-disengage	False parry-real parry riposte	

Notes:

Observed on:					
Opponent:					
Who won?					
Score					

Name:					Country/Division:	
Club:						
Age group:	Y10	Y12	Y14	CDT	JNR	OPEN	VET
Visuals:	Righty	Lefty	Taller		Shorter	Growing
Trends:	Attacker	Defender	Counter attacker			
Tactics:	Tactical	Sometimes Tactical		Not Very Tactical		
Timing:	Slow/Quick			Poor/Good Timing		
	Awkward Timing			Arrhythmic Timing		

Opponent In the Box:	Attack in Prep	Varies target
Closeout	Beat attacks	Parry-Riposte
Feint deceive	Counter Attack with (timing)(closeout)	
Big steps	Pull Distance (make me fall short)	Other:

Opponent Attacks:	Simple	Composed	Long smooth attacks
Big steps	Small steps	Beat attacks	Strong Blade Actions
Search + Take Blade	Feint deceive (lateral)(circular)		
Counter Attack (timing)(body displacement)(opposition):			

Opponent Defense:	Parry: 2 3 4 5	Circle: 2 3 4
Sweeping parries while retreating	Counter time	2 parries

Actions that worked:	Parry riposte 2 3 4 5	Circle: 2 3 4
Pull distance – make opp fall short	Push and attack	Pull and defend
Feint deceive (4-6) (circle 3) (around 2) ( ) ( )		
Beat-disengage	False parry-real parry riposte	

Notes:

Observed on:					
Opponent:					
Who won?					
Score					

C

Name:				Country/Division:	
Club:					
Age group:	Y10	Y12	Y14	CDT	JNR	OPEN	VET
Visuals:	Righty	Lefty	Taller	Shorter	Growing
Trends:	Attacker	Defender	Counter attacker	
Tactics:	Tactical	Sometimes Tactical	Not Very Tactical	
Timing:	Slow/Quick		Poor/Good Timing	
	Awkward Timing		Arrhythmic Timing	

Opponent In the Box:	Attack in Prep	Varies target
Closeout	Beat attacks	Parry-Riposte
Feint deceive	Counter Attack with (timing)(closeout)	
Big steps	Pull Distance (make me fall short)	Other:

Opponent Attacks:	Simple	Composed	Long smooth attacks
Big steps	Small steps	Beat attacks	Strong Blade Actions
Search + Take Blade	Feint deceive (lateral)(circular)		
Counter Attack (timing)(body displacement)(opposition):			

Opponent Defense:	Parry: 2 3 4 5	Circle: 2 3 4	
Sweeping parries while retreating	Counter time		2 parries

Actions that worked:	Parry riposte 2 3 4 5	Circle: 2 3 4
Pull distance – make opp fall short	Push and attack	Pull and defend
Feint deceive (4-6) (circle 3) (around 2) (	) (	)
Beat-disengage	False parry-real parry riposte	

Notes:	

Observed on:					
Opponent:					
Who won?					
Score					

Name:					Country/Division:		
Club:							
Age group:	Y10	Y12	Y14	CDT	JNR	OPEN	VET
Visuals:	Righty	Lefty	Taller		Shorter		Growing
Trends:	Attacker	Defender	Counter attacker				
Tactics:	Tactical	Sometimes Tactical			Not Very Tactical		
Timing:	Slow/Quick				Poor/Good Timing		
	Awkward Timing				Arrhythmic Timing		

Opponent In the Box:	Attack in Prep	Varies target
Closeout	Beat attacks	Parry-Riposte
Feint deceive	Counter Attack with (timing)(closeout)	
Big steps	Pull Distance (make me fall short)	Other:

Opponent Attacks:	Simple	Composed	Long smooth attacks
Big steps	Small steps	Beat attacks	Strong Blade Actions
Search + Take Blade	Feint deceive (lateral)(circular)		
Counter Attack (timing)(body displacement)(opposition):			

Opponent Defense:	Parry: 2 3 4 5	Circle: 2 3 4
Sweeping parries while retreating	Counter time	2 parries

Actions that worked:	Parry riposte 2 3 4 5	Circle: 2 3 4
Pull distance – make opp fall short	Push and attack	Pull and defend
Feint deceive (4-6) (circle 3) (around 2) ( ) ( )		
Beat-disengage	False parry-real parry riposte	

Notes:

Observed on:				
Opponent:				
Who won?				
Score				

C

C

Name:		Country/Division:	
Club:			
Age group:	Y10 Y12 Y14 CDT JNR OPEN VET		
Visuals:	Righty	Lefty	Taller	Shorter	Growing
Trends:	Attacker	Defender	Counter attacker	
Tactics:	Tactical	Sometimes Tactical	Not Very Tactical	

Timing:	Slow/Quick	Poor/Good Timing
	Awkward Timing	Arrhythmic Timing

Opponent In the Box:	Attack in Prep	Varies target
Closeout	Beat attacks	Parry-Riposte
Feint deceive	Counter Attack with (timing)(closeout)	
Big steps	Pull Distance (make me fall short)	Other:

Opponent Attacks:	Simple	Composed	Long smooth attacks
Big steps	Small steps	Beat attacks	Strong Blade Actions
Search + Take Blade	Feint deceive (lateral)(circular)		
Counter Attack (timing)(body displacement)(opposition):			

Opponent Defense:	Parry: 2 3 4 5	Circle: 2 3 4
Sweeping parries while retreating	Counter time	2 parries

Actions that worked:	Parry riposte 2 3 4 5	Circle: 2 3 4
Pull distance – make opp fall short	Push and attack	Pull and defend
Feint deceive (4-6) (circle 3) (around 2) (	) (	)
Beat-disengage	False parry-real parry riposte	

Notes:	

Observed on:					
Opponent:					
Who won?					
Score					

Name:					Country/Division:		
Club:							
Age group:	Y10	Y12	Y14	CDT	JNR	OPEN	VET
Visuals:	Righty	Lefty	Taller		Shorter		Growing
Trends:	Attacker	Defender	Counter attacker				
Tactics:	Tactical	Sometimes Tactical			Not Very Tactical		
Timing:	Slow/Quick			Poor/Good Timing			
	Awkward Timing			Arrhythmic Timing			

D

Opponent In the Box:	Attack in Prep		Varies target	
Closeout	Beat attacks		Parry-Riposte	
Feint deceive	Counter Attack with (timing)(closeout)			
Big steps	Pull Distance (make me fall short)		Other:	

Opponent Attacks:	Simple	Composed	Long smooth attacks
Big steps	Small steps	Beat attacks	Strong Blade Actions
Search + Take Blade	Feint deceive (lateral)(circular)		
Counter Attack (timing)(body displacement)(opposition):			

Opponent Defense:	Parry: 2 3 4 5	Circle: 2 3 4	
Sweeping parries while retreating	Counter time		2 parries

Actions that worked:	Parry riposte 2 3 4 5	Circle: 2 3 4	
Pull distance – make opp fall short		Push and attack	Pull and defend
Feint deceive (4-6) (circle 3) (around 2) (	) (		)
Beat-disengage	False parry-real parry riposte		

Notes:

Observed on:					
Opponent:					
Who won?					
Score					

D

Name:		Country/Division:	
Club:			

Age group:	Y10	Y12	Y14	CDT	JNR	OPEN	VET
Visuals:	Righty	Lefty	Taller		Shorter		Growing
Trends:	Attacker	Defender	Counter attacker				
Tactics:	Tactical	Sometimes Tactical		Not Very Tactical			
Timing:	Slow/Quick			Poor/Good Timing			
	Awkward Timing			Arrhythmic Timing			

Opponent In the Box:		Attack in Prep		Varies target	
Closeout		Beat attacks		Parry-Riposte	
Feint deceive		Counter Attack with (timing)(closeout)			
Big steps	Pull Distance (make me fall short)			Other:	
Opponent Attacks:		Simple	Composed	Long smooth attacks	
Big steps	Small steps	Beat attacks		Strong Blade Actions	
Search + Take Blade		Feint deceive (lateral)(circular)			
Counter Attack (timing)(body displacement)(opposition):					
Opponent Defense:		Parry: 2 3 4 5		Circle: 2 3 4	
Sweeping parries while retreating		Counter time			2 parries
Actions that worked:		Parry riposte 2 3 4 5		Circle: 2 3 4	
Pull distance – make opp fall short			Push and attack	Pull and defend	
Feint deceive (4-6) (circle 3) (around 2) (			) (	)	
Beat-disengage		False parry-real parry riposte			

Notes:	

Observed on:					
Opponent:					
Who won?					
Score					

Name:					Country/Division:		
Club:							
Age group:	Y10	Y12	Y14	CDT	JNR	OPEN	VET
Visuals:	Righty	Lefty	Taller		Shorter		Growing
Trends:	Attacker	Defender	Counter attacker				
Tactics:	Tactical	Sometimes Tactical			Not Very Tactical		
Timing:	Slow/Quick			Poor/Good Timing			
	Awkward Timing			Arrhythmic Timing			

D

Opponent In the Box:		Attack in Prep		Varies target	
Closeout		Beat attacks		Parry-Riposte	
Feint deceive		Counter Attack with (timing)(closeout)			
Big steps	Pull Distance (make me fall short)			Other:	
Opponent Attacks:		Simple	Composed	Long smooth attacks	
Big steps	Small steps	Beat attacks		Strong Blade Actions	
Search + Take Blade		Feint deceive (lateral)(circular)			
Counter Attack (timing)(body displacement)(opposition):					
Opponent Defense:		Parry: 2 3 4 5		Circle: 2 3 4	
Sweeping parries while retreating		Counter time			2 parries
Actions that worked:		Parry riposte 2 3 4 5		Circle: 2 3 4	
Pull distance – make opp fall short			Push and attack	Pull and defend	
Feint deceive (4-6) (circle 3) (around 2) ( ) ( )					
Beat-disengage		False parry-real parry riposte			

Notes:					
Observed on:					
Opponent:					
Who won?					
Score					

D

Name:		Country/Division:	
Club:			

Age group:	Y10	Y12	Y14	CDT	JNR	OPEN	VET
Visuals:	Righty	Lefty		Taller		Shorter	Growing
Trends:	Attacker		Defender	Counter attacker			
Tactics:	Tactical		Sometimes Tactical		Not Very Tactical		
Timing:	Slow/Quick				Poor/Good Timing		
	Awkward Timing				Arrhythmic Timing		

Opponent In the Box:		Attack in Prep		Varies target	
Closeout		Beat attacks		Parry-Riposte	
Feint deceive		Counter Attack with (timing)(closeout)			
Big steps		Pull Distance (make me fall short)		Other:	
Opponent Attacks:		Simple	Composed	Long smooth attacks	
Big steps	Small steps	Beat attacks		Strong Blade Actions	
Search + Take Blade		Feint deceive (lateral)(circular)			
Counter Attack (timing)(body displacement)(opposition):					
Opponent Defense:		Parry: 2 3 4 5		Circle: 2 3 4	
Sweeping parries while retreating		Counter time		2 parries	
Actions that worked:		Parry riposte 2 3 4 5		Circle: 2 3 4	
Pull distance – make opp fall short			Push and attack	Pull and defend	
Feint deceive (4-6) (circle 3) (around 2) (			) (	)	
Beat-disengage		False parry-real parry riposte			

Notes:	

Observed on:					
Opponent:					
Who won?					
Score					

Name:					Country/Division:	
Club:						
Age group:	Y10	Y12	Y14	CDT	JNR OPEN	VET
Visuals:	Righty	Lefty	Taller		Shorter	Growing
Trends:	Attacker	Defender	Counter attacker			
Tactics:	Tactical	Sometimes Tactical			Not Very Tactical	
Timing:	Slow/Quick			Poor/Good Timing		
	Awkward Timing			Arrhythmic Timing		

D

Opponent In the Box:	Attack in Prep		Varies target	
Closeout	Beat attacks		Parry-Riposte	
Feint deceive	Counter Attack with (timing)(closeout)			
Big steps	Pull Distance (make me fall short)		Other:	
Opponent Attacks:	Simple	Composed	Long smooth attacks	
Big steps	Small steps	Beat attacks	Strong Blade Actions	
Search + Take Blade	Feint deceive (lateral)(circular)			
Counter Attack (timing)(body displacement)(opposition):				
Opponent Defense:	Parry: 2 3 4 5		Circle: 2 3 4	
Sweeping parries while retreating	Counter time		2 parries	
Actions that worked:	Parry riposte 2 3 4 5		Circle: 2 3 4	
Pull distance – make opp fall short		Push and attack	Pull and defend	
Feint deceive (4-6) (circle 3) (around 2) ( ) ( )				
Beat-disengage	False parry-real parry riposte			

Notes:

Observed on:				
Opponent:				
Who won?				
Score				

D

Name:					Country/Division:	
Club:						
Age group:	Y10	Y12	Y14	CDT	JNR	OPEN	VET
Visuals:	Righty	Lefty	Taller		Shorter	Growing
Trends:	Attacker	Defender	Counter attacker			
Tactics:	Tactical	Sometimes Tactical		Not Very Tactical		
Timing:	Slow/Quick		Poor/Good Timing			
	Awkward Timing		Arrhythmic Timing			

Opponent In the Box:		Attack in Prep	Varies target	
Closeout		Beat attacks	Parry-Riposte	
Feint deceive		Counter Attack with (timing)(closeout)		
Big steps	Pull Distance (make me fall short)		Other:	
Opponent Attacks:		Simple	Composed	Long smooth attacks
Big steps	Small steps	Beat attacks		Strong Blade Actions
Search + Take Blade		Feint deceive (lateral)(circular)		
Counter Attack (timing)(body displacement)(opposition):				
Opponent Defense:		Parry: 2 3 4 5	Circle: 2 3 4	
Sweeping parries while retreating		Counter time		2 parries
Actions that worked:		Parry riposte 2 3 4 5	Circle: 2 3 4	
Pull distance – make opp fall short			Push and attack	Pull and defend
Feint deceive (4-6) (circle 3) (around 2) (		) (	)	
Beat-disengage		False parry-real parry riposte		
Notes:				

Observed on:					
Opponent:					
Who won?					
Score					

Name:						Country/Division:	
Club:							
Age group:	Y10	Y12	Y14	CDT	JNR	OPEN	VET
Visuals:	Righty	Lefty	Taller		Shorter		Growing
Trends:	Attacker	Defender	Counter attacker				
Tactics:	Tactical	Sometimes Tactical			Not Very Tactical		
Timing:	Slow/Quick			Poor/Good Timing			
	Awkward Timing			Arrhythmic Timing			

Opponent In the Box:	Attack in Prep		Varies target	
Closeout		Beat attacks		Parry-Riposte
Feint deceive		Counter Attack with (timing)(closeout)		
Big steps	Pull Distance (make me fall short)		Other:	

Opponent Attacks:	Simple	Composed	Long smooth attacks
Big steps	Small steps	Beat attacks	Strong Blade Actions
Search + Take Blade	Feint deceive (lateral)(circular)		
Counter Attack (timing)(body displacement)(opposition):			

Opponent Defense:	Parry: 2 3 4 5	Circle: 2 3 4
Sweeping parries while retreating	Counter time	2 parries

Actions that worked:	Parry riposte 2 3 4 5	Circle: 2 3 4
Pull distance – make opp fall short	Push and attack	Pull and defend
Feint deceive (4-6) (circle 3) (around 2) ( ) ( )		
Beat-disengage	False parry-real parry riposte	

Notes:					
Observed on:					
Opponent:					
Who won?					
Score					

E

E

Name:					Country/Division:	
Club:						
Age group:	Y10	Y12	Y14	CDT	JNR	OPEN	VET
Visuals:	Righty	Lefty	Taller		Shorter	Growing
Trends:	Attacker	Defender	Counter attacker			
Tactics:	Tactical	Sometimes Tactical		Not Very Tactical		
Timing:	Slow/Quick			Poor/Good Timing		
	Awkward Timing			Arrhythmic Timing		

Opponent In the Box:		Attack in Prep	Varies target	
Closeout		Beat attacks	Parry-Riposte	
Feint deceive		Counter Attack with (timing)(closeout)		
Big steps	Pull Distance (make me fall short)		Other:	
Opponent Attacks:		Simple	Composed	Long smooth attacks
Big steps	Small steps	Beat attacks		Strong Blade Actions
Search + Take Blade		Feint deceive (lateral)(circular)		
Counter Attack (timing)(body displacement)(opposition):				
Opponent Defense:		Parry: 2 3 4 5	Circle: 2 3 4	
Sweeping parries while retreating		Counter time		2 parries
Actions that worked:		Parry riposte 2 3 4 5	Circle: 2 3 4	
Pull distance – make opp fall short		Push and attack	Pull and defend	
Feint deceive (4-6) (circle 3) (around 2) (		) (	)	
Beat-disengage		False parry-real parry riposte		

Notes:

Observed on:					
Opponent:					
Who won?					
Score					

Name:						Country/Division:	
Club:							
Age group:	Y10	Y12	Y14	CDT	JNR	OPEN	VET
Visuals:	Righty	Lefty		Taller		Shorter	Growing
Trends:	Attacker	Defender		Counter attacker			
Tactics:	Tactical	Sometimes Tactical				Not Very Tactical	
Timing:	Slow/Quick				Poor/Good Timing		
	Awkward Timing				Arrhythmic Timing		

Opponent In the Box:	Attack in Prep		Varies target	
Closeout	Beat attacks		Parry-Riposte	
Feint deceive	Counter Attack with (timing)(closeout)			
Big steps	Pull Distance (make me fall short)		Other:	

Opponent Attacks:		Simple	Composed	Long smooth attacks
Big steps	Small steps	Beat attacks		Strong Blade Actions
Search + Take Blade	Feint deceive (lateral)(circular)			
Counter Attack (timing)(body displacement)(opposition):				

Opponent Defense:	Parry: 2 3 4 5		Circle: 2 3 4	
Sweeping parries while retreating		Counter time		2 parries

Actions that worked:	Parry riposte 2 3 4 5		Circle: 2 3 4	
Pull distance – make opp fall short		Push and attack		Pull and defend
Feint deceive (4-6) (circle 3) (around 2) ( ) ( )				
Beat-disengage	False parry-real parry riposte			

Notes:

Observed on:				
Opponent:				
Who won?				
Score				

E

E

Name:					Country/Division:		
Club:							
Age group:	Y10	Y12	Y14	CDT	JNR	OPEN	VET
Visuals:	Righty	Lefty	Taller		Shorter		Growing
Trends:	Attacker	Defender	Counter attacker				
Tactics:	Tactical	Sometimes Tactical			Not Very Tactical		
Timing:	Slow/Quick				Poor/Good Timing		
	Awkward Timing				Arrhythmic Timing		

Opponent In the Box:		Attack in Prep		Varies target	
Closeout		Beat attacks		Parry-Riposte	
Feint deceive		Counter Attack with (timing)(closeout)			
Big steps	Pull Distance (make me fall short)			Other:	
Opponent Attacks:		Simple	Composed	Long smooth attacks	
Big steps	Small steps	Beat attacks		Strong Blade Actions	
Search + Take Blade		Feint deceive (lateral)(circular)			
Counter Attack (timing)(body displacement)(opposition):					
Opponent Defense:		Parry: 2 3 4 5		Circle: 2 3 4	
Sweeping parries while retreating		Counter time			2 parries
Actions that worked:		Parry riposte 2 3 4 5		Circle: 2 3 4	
Pull distance – make opp fall short			Push and attack	Pull and defend	
Feint deceive (4-6) (circle 3) (around 2) ( ) ( )					
Beat-disengage		False parry-real parry riposte			

Notes:							
Observed on:							
Opponent:							
Who won?							
Score							

Name:						Country/Division:	
Club:							
Age group:	Y10	Y12	Y14	CDT	JNR	OPEN	VET
Visuals:	Righty	Lefty	Taller		Shorter		Growing
Trends:	Attacker	Defender	Counter attacker				
Tactics:	Tactical	Sometimes Tactical			Not Very Tactical		
Timing:	Slow/Quick			Poor/Good Timing			
	Awkward Timing			Arrhythmic Timing			

F

Opponent In the Box:	Attack in Prep		Varies target	
Closeout	Beat attacks		Parry-Riposte	
Feint deceive	Counter Attack with (timing)(closeout)			
Big steps	Pull Distance (make me fall short)		Other:	
Opponent Attacks:	Simple	Composed	Long smooth attacks	
Big steps	Small steps	Beat attacks	Strong Blade Actions	
Search + Take Blade	Feint deceive (lateral)(circular)			
Counter Attack (timing)(body displacement)(opposition):				
Opponent Defense:	Parry: 2 3 4 5		Circle: 2 3 4	
Sweeping parries while retreating		Counter time		2 parries
Actions that worked:	Parry riposte 2 3 4 5		Circle: 2 3 4	
Pull distance – make opp fall short		Push and attack	Pull and defend	
Feint deceive (4-6) (circle 3) (around 2) ( ) ( )				
Beat-disengage	False parry-real parry riposte			
Notes:				

Observed on:					
Opponent:					
Who won?					
Score					

F

Name:		Country/Division:	
Club:			

Age group:	Y10	Y12	Y14	CDT	JNR	OPEN	VET
Visuals:	Righty	Lefty	Taller		Shorter		Growing
Trends:	Attacker	Defender	Counter attacker				
Tactics:	Tactical	Sometimes Tactical		Not Very Tactical			
Timing:	Slow/Quick			Poor/Good Timing			
	Awkward Timing			Arrhythmic Timing			

Opponent In the Box:		Attack in Prep		Varies target	
Closeout		Beat attacks		Parry-Riposte	
Feint deceive		Counter Attack with (timing)(closeout)			
Big steps	Pull Distance (make me fall short)			Other:	
Opponent Attacks:		Simple	Composed	Long smooth attacks	
Big steps	Small steps	Beat attacks		Strong Blade Actions	
Search + Take Blade		Feint deceive (lateral)(circular)			
Counter Attack (timing)(body displacement)(opposition):					
Opponent Defense:		Parry: 2 3 4 5		Circle: 2 3 4	
Sweeping parries while retreating		Counter time			2 parries
Actions that worked:		Parry riposte 2 3 4 5		Circle: 2 3 4	
Pull distance – make opp fall short			Push and attack	Pull and defend	
Feint deceive (4-6) (circle 3) (around 2) ( ) ( )					
Beat-disengage		False parry-real parry riposte			

Notes:	

Observed on:					
Opponent:					
Who won?					
Score					

Name:		Country/Division:	
Club:			

Age group:	Y10	Y12	Y14	CDT	JNR	OPEN	VET
Visuals:	Righty	Lefty	Taller		Shorter		Growing
Trends:	Attacker	Defender	Counter attacker				
Tactics:	Tactical	Sometimes Tactical			Not Very Tactical		
Timing:	Slow/Quick			Poor/Good Timing			
	Awkward Timing			Arrhythmic Timing			

F

Opponent In the Box:	Attack in Prep	Varies target
Closeout	Beat attacks	Parry-Riposte
Feint deceive	Counter Attack with (timing)(closeout)	
Big steps	Pull Distance (make me fall short)	Other:

Opponent Attacks:		Simple	Composed	Long smooth attacks
Big steps	Small steps	Beat attacks		Strong Blade Actions
Search + Take Blade	Feint deceive (lateral)(circular)			
Counter Attack (timing)(body displacement)(opposition):				

Opponent Defense:	Parry: 2 3 4 5	Circle: 2 3 4
Sweeping parries while retreating	Counter time	2 parries

Actions that worked:	Parry riposte 2 3 4 5	Circle: 2 3 4
Pull distance – make opp fall short	Push and attack	Pull and defend
Feint deceive (4-6) (circle 3) (around 2) ( ) ( )		
Beat-disengage	False parry-real parry riposte	

Notes:

Observed on:					
Opponent:					
Who won?					
Score					

F

Name:					Country/Division:	
Club:						
Age group:	Y10	Y12	Y14	CDT	JNR	OPEN	VET
Visuals:	Righty	Lefty	Taller	Shorter	Growing
Trends:	Attacker	Defender	Counter attacker		
Tactics:	Tactical	Sometimes Tactical	Not Very Tactical		
Timing:	Slow/Quick		Poor/Good Timing		
	Awkward Timing		Arrhythmic Timing		

Opponent In the Box:	Attack in Prep	Varies target
Closeout	Beat attacks	Parry-Riposte
Feint deceive	Counter Attack with (timing)(closeout)	
Big steps	Pull Distance (make me fall short)	Other:

Opponent Attacks:		Simple	Composed	Long smooth attacks
Big steps	Small steps	Beat attacks		Strong Blade Actions
Search + Take Blade		Feint deceive (lateral)(circular)		
Counter Attack (timing)(body displacement)(opposition):				

Opponent Defense:	Parry: 2 3 4 5	Circle: 2 3 4
Sweeping parries while retreating	Counter time	2 parries

Actions that worked:	Parry riposte 2 3 4 5	Circle: 2 3 4
Pull distance – make opp fall short	Push and attack	Pull and defend
Feint deceive (4-6) (circle 3) (around 2) ( ) ( )		
Beat-disengage	False parry-real parry riposte	

Notes:	

Observed on:					
Opponent:					
Who won?					
Score					

Name:				Country/Division:	
Club:					
Age group:	Y10	Y12	Y14	CDT	JNR OPEN VET
Visuals:	Righty	Lefty	Taller	Shorter	Growing
Trends:	Attacker	Defender	Counter attacker		
Tactics:	Tactical	Sometimes Tactical		Not Very Tactical	
Timing:	Slow/Quick			Poor/Good Timing	
	Awkward Timing			Arrhythmic Timing	

Opponent In the Box:	Attack in Prep	Varies target
Closeout	Beat attacks	Parry-Riposte
Feint deceive	Counter Attack with (timing)(closeout)
Big steps	Pull Distance (make me fall short)	Other:

Opponent Attacks:	Simple	Composed	Long smooth attacks
Big steps	Small steps	Beat attacks	Strong Blade Actions
Search + Take Blade	Feint deceive (lateral)(circular)	
Counter Attack (timing)(body displacement)(opposition):		

Opponent Defense:	Parry: 2 3 4 5	Circle: 2 3 4
Sweeping parries while retreating	Counter time	2 parries

Actions that worked:	Parry riposte 2 3 4 5	Circle: 2 3 4
Pull distance – make opp fall short	Push and attack	Pull and defend
Feint deceive (4-6) (circle 3) (around 2) ( ) ( )	
Beat-disengage	False parry-real parry riposte

Notes:

Observed on:				
Opponent:				
Who won?				
Score				

G

Name:					Country/Division:	
Club:						
Age group:	Y10	Y12	Y14	CDT	JNR	OPEN	VET
Visuals:	Righty	Lefty	Taller		Shorter	Growing
Trends:	Attacker	Defender	Counter attacker			
Tactics:	Tactical	Sometimes Tactical		Not Very Tactical		
Timing:	Slow/Quick		Poor/Good Timing			
	Awkward Timing		Arrhythmic Timing			

G

Opponent In the Box:		Attack in Prep	Varies target	
Closeout		Beat attacks	Parry-Riposte	
Feint deceive		Counter Attack with (timing)(closeout)		
Big steps	Pull Distance (make me fall short)		Other:	
Opponent Attacks:		Simple	Composed	Long smooth attacks
Big steps	Small steps	Beat attacks		Strong Blade Actions
Search + Take Blade		Feint deceive (lateral)(circular)		
Counter Attack (timing)(body displacement)(opposition):				
Opponent Defense:		Parry: 2 3 4 5	Circle: 2 3 4	
Sweeping parries while retreating		Counter time		2 parries
Actions that worked:		Parry riposte 2 3 4 5	Circle: 2 3 4	
Pull distance – make opp fall short		Push and attack	Pull and defend	
Feint deceive (4-6) (circle 3) (around 2) (		) (	)	
Beat-disengage		False parry-real parry riposte		
Notes:				
Observed on:					
Opponent:					
Who won?					
Score					

Name:					Country/Division:		
Club:							
Age group:	Y10	Y12	Y14	CDT	JNR	OPEN	VET
Visuals:	Righty	Lefty	Taller		Shorter		Growing
Trends:	Attacker	Defender	Counter attacker				
Tactics:	Tactical	Sometimes Tactical			Not Very Tactical		
Timing:	Slow/Quick			Poor/Good Timing			
	Awkward Timing			Arrhythmic Timing			

Opponent In the Box:	Attack in Prep		Varies target	
Closeout	Beat attacks		Parry-Riposte	
Feint deceive	Counter Attack with (timing)(closeout)			
Big steps	Pull Distance (make me fall short)		Other:	

Opponent Attacks:	Simple		Composed	Long smooth attacks
Big steps	Small steps	Beat attacks		Strong Blade Actions
Search + Take Blade	Feint deceive (lateral)(circular)			
Counter Attack (timing)(body displacement)(opposition):				

Opponent Defense:	Parry: 2 3 4 5		Circle: 2 3 4	
Sweeping parries while retreating		Counter time		2 parries

Actions that worked:	Parry riposte 2 3 4 5	Circle: 2 3 4
Pull distance – make opp fall short	Push and attack	Pull and defend
Feint deceive (4-6) (circle 3) (around 2) ( ) ( )		
Beat-disengage	False parry-real parry riposte	

Notes:

Observed on:					
Opponent:					
Who won?					
Score					

G

G

Name:				Country/Division:	
Club:					
Age group:	Y10	Y12	Y14	CDT	JNR	OPEN	VET
Visuals:	Righty	Lefty	Taller	Shorter	Growing
Trends:	Attacker	Defender	Counter attacker		
Tactics:	Tactical	Sometimes Tactical	Not Very Tactical		
Timing:	Slow/Quick		Poor/Good Timing		
	Awkward Timing		Arrhythmic Timing		
Opponent In the Box:	Attack in Prep		Varies target		
Closeout	Beat attacks		Parry-Riposte		
Feint deceive	Counter Attack with (timing)(closeout)				
Big steps	Pull Distance (make me fall short)		Other:		
Opponent Attacks:	Simple	Composed	Long smooth attacks		
Big steps	Small steps	Beat attacks	Strong Blade Actions		
Search + Take Blade	Feint deceive (lateral)(circular)				
Counter Attack (timing)(body displacement)(opposition):					
Opponent Defense:	Parry: 2 3 4 5		Circle: 2 3 4		
Sweeping parries while retreating	Counter time		2 parries		
Actions that worked:	Parry riposte 2 3 4 5		Circle: 2 3 4		
Pull distance – make opp fall short		Push and attack	Pull and defend		
Feint deceive (4-6) (circle 3) (around 2) ( ) ( )					
Beat-disengage	False parry-real parry riposte				
Notes:					
Observed on:					
Opponent:					
Who won?					
Score					

Name:			Country/Division:	
Club:				
Age group:	Y10 Y12 Y14		CDT JNR OPEN VET	
Visuals:	Righty	Lefty	Taller	Shorter	Growing
Trends:	Attacker	Defender	Counter attacker	
Tactics:	Tactical	Sometimes Tactical	Not Very Tactical	
Timing:	Slow/Quick		Poor/Good Timing	
	Awkward Timing		Arrhythmic Timing	

G

Opponent In the Box:	Attack in Prep	Varies target
Closeout	Beat attacks	Parry-Riposte
Feint deceive	Counter Attack with (timing)(closeout)	
Big steps	Pull Distance (make me fall short)	Other:

Opponent Attacks:	Simple	Composed	Long smooth attacks
Big steps	Small steps	Beat attacks	Strong Blade Actions
Search + Take Blade	Feint deceive (lateral)(circular)		
Counter Attack (timing)(body displacement)(opposition):			

Opponent Defense:	Parry: 2 3 4 5	Circle: 2 3 4
Sweeping parries while retreating	Counter time	2 parries

Actions that worked:	Parry riposte 2 3 4 5	Circle: 2 3 4
Pull distance – make opp fall short	Push and attack	Pull and defend
Feint deceive (4-6) (circle 3) (around 2) ( ) ( )		
Beat-disengage	False parry-real parry riposte	

Notes:

Observed on:					
Opponent:					
Who won?					
Score					

Name:					Country/Division:		
Club:							
Age group:	Y10	Y12	Y14	CDT	JNR	OPEN	VET
Visuals:	Righty	Lefty		Taller		Shorter	Growing
Trends:	Attacker	Defender		Counter attacker			
Tactics:	Tactical	Sometimes Tactical			Not Very Tactical		
Timing:	Slow/Quick				Poor/Good Timing		
	Awkward Timing				Arrhythmic Timing		

Opponent In the Box:		Attack in Prep		Varies target	
Closeout		Beat attacks		Parry-Riposte	
Feint deceive		Counter Attack with (timing)(closeout)			
Big steps	Pull Distance (make me fall short)			Other:	
Opponent Attacks:		Simple	Composed	Long smooth attacks	
Big steps	Small steps	Beat attacks		Strong Blade Actions	
Search + Take Blade		Feint deceive (lateral)(circular)			
Counter Attack (timing)(body displacement)(opposition):					
Opponent Defense:		Parry: 2 3 4 5		Circle: 2 3 4	
Sweeping parries while retreating		Counter time		2 parries	
Actions that worked:		Parry riposte 2 3 4 5		Circle: 2 3 4	
Pull distance – make opp fall short		Push and attack		Pull and defend	
Feint deceive (4-6) (circle 3) (around 2) (		) (	)		
Beat-disengage		False parry-real parry riposte			
Notes:					

Observed on:					
Opponent:					
Who won?					
Score					

G

Name:					Country/Division:	
Club:						
Age group:	Y10	Y12	Y14	CDT	JNR OPEN	VET
Visuals:	Righty	Lefty	Taller		Shorter	Growing
Trends:	Attacker	Defender	Counter attacker			
Tactics:	Tactical	Sometimes Tactical			Not Very Tactical	
Timing:	Slow/Quick			Poor/Good Timing		
	Awkward Timing			Arrhythmic Timing		

Opponent In the Box:	Attack in Prep		Varies target	
Closeout	Beat attacks		Parry-Riposte	
Feint deceive	Counter Attack with (timing)(closeout)			
Big steps	Pull Distance (make me fall short)		Other:	
Opponent Attacks:	Simple	Composed	Long smooth attacks	
Big steps	Small steps	Beat attacks	Strong Blade Actions	
Search + Take Blade	Feint deceive (lateral)(circular)			
Counter Attack (timing)(body displacement)(opposition):				
Opponent Defense:	Parry: 2 3 4 5		Circle: 2 3 4	
Sweeping parries while retreating	Counter time		2 parries	
Actions that worked:	Parry riposte 2 3 4 5		Circle: 2 3 4	
Pull distance – make opp fall short		Push and attack	Pull and defend	
Feint deceive (4-6) (circle 3) (around 2) ( ) ( )				
Beat-disengage	False parry-real parry riposte			

Notes:	

Observed on:					
Opponent:					
Who won?					
Score					

H

H

Name:				Country/Division:	
Club:					
Age group:	Y10	Y12	Y14	CDT	JNR	OPEN	VET
Visuals:	Righty	Lefty	Taller	Shorter	Growing
Trends:	Attacker	Defender	Counter attacker		
Tactics:	Tactical	Sometimes Tactical	Not Very Tactical		
Timing:	Slow/Quick		Poor/Good Timing		
	Awkward Timing		Arrhythmic Timing		

Opponent In the Box:	Attack in Prep	Varies target
Closeout	Beat attacks	Parry-Riposte
Feint deceive	Counter Attack with (timing)(closeout)	
Big steps	Pull Distance (make me fall short)	Other:

Opponent Attacks:		Simple	Composed	Long smooth attacks
Big steps	Small steps	Beat attacks		Strong Blade Actions
Search + Take Blade		Feint deceive (lateral)(circular)		
Counter Attack (timing)(body displacement)(opposition):				

Opponent Defense:	Parry: 2 3 4 5	Circle: 2 3 4
Sweeping parries while retreating	Counter time	2 parries

Actions that worked:	Parry riposte 2 3 4 5	Circle: 2 3 4
Pull distance – make opp fall short	Push and attack	Pull and defend
Feint deceive (4-6) (circle 3) (around 2) ( ) ( )		
Beat-disengage	False parry-real parry riposte	

Notes:

Observed on:				
Opponent:				
Who won?				
Score				

Name:					Country/Division:		
Club:							
Age group:	Y10	Y12	Y14	CDT	JNR	OPEN	VET
Visuals:	Righty	Lefty	Taller		Shorter		Growing
Trends:	Attacker	Defender	Counter attacker				
Tactics:	Tactical	Sometimes Tactical			Not Very Tactical		
Timing:	Slow/Quick			Poor/Good Timing			
	Awkward Timing			Arrhythmic Timing			

Opponent In the Box:	Attack in Prep		Varies target	
Closeout	Beat attacks		Parry-Riposte	
Feint deceive	Counter Attack with (timing)(closeout)			
Big steps	Pull Distance (make me fall short)		Other:	

Opponent Attacks:	Simple	Composed	Long smooth attacks
Big steps	Small steps	Beat attacks	Strong Blade Actions
Search + Take Blade	Feint deceive (lateral)(circular)		
Counter Attack (timing)(body displacement)(opposition):			

Opponent Defense:	Parry: 2 3 4 5	Circle: 2 3 4	
Sweeping parries while retreating	Counter time		2 parries

Actions that worked:	Parry riposte 2 3 4 5	Circle: 2 3 4	
Pull distance – make opp fall short		Push and attack	Pull and defend
Feint deceive (4-6) (circle 3) (around 2) (	) (	)	
Beat-disengage	False parry-real parry riposte		

Notes:

Observed on:				
Opponent:				
Who won?				
Score				

H

Name:					Country/Division:		
Club:							
Age group:	Y10	Y12	Y14	CDT	JNR	OPEN	VET
Visuals:	Righty	Lefty	Taller		Shorter		Growing
Trends:	Attacker	Defender	Counter attacker				
Tactics:	Tactical	Sometimes Tactical			Not Very Tactical		
Timing:	Slow/Quick			Poor/Good Timing			
	Awkward Timing			Arrhythmic Timing			

Opponent In the Box:		Attack in Prep		Varies target		
Closeout		Beat attacks		Parry-Riposte		
Feint deceive		Counter Attack with (timing)(closeout)				
Big steps		Pull Distance (make me fall short)			Other:	
Opponent Attacks:		Simple	Composed	Long smooth attacks		
Big steps	Small steps	Beat attacks		Strong Blade Actions		
Search + Take Blade		Feint deceive (lateral)(circular)				
Counter Attack (timing)(body displacement)(opposition):						
Opponent Defense:		Parry: 2 3 4 5		Circle: 2 3 4		
Sweeping parries while retreating		Counter time			2 parries	
Actions that worked:		Parry riposte 2 3 4 5		Circle: 2 3 4		
Pull distance – make opp fall short			Push and attack	Pull and defend		
Feint deceive (4-6) (circle 3) (around 2) ( ) ( )						
Beat-disengage		False parry-real parry riposte				
Notes:						
Observed on:						
Opponent:						
Who won?						
Score						

H

Name:					Country/Division:	
Club:						
Age group:	Y10	Y12	Y14	CDT	JNR OPEN	VET
Visuals:	Righty	Lefty	Taller		Shorter	Growing
Trends:	Attacker	Defender	Counter attacker			
Tactics:	Tactical	Sometimes Tactical			Not Very Tactical	
Timing:	Slow/Quick			Poor/Good Timing		
	Awkward Timing			Arrhythmic Timing		

Opponent In the Box:	Attack in Prep	Varies target
Closeout	Beat attacks	Parry-Riposte
Feint deceive	Counter Attack with (timing)(closeout)	
Big steps	Pull Distance (make me fall short)	Other:

Opponent Attacks:		Simple	Composed	Long smooth attacks
Big steps	Small steps	Beat attacks		Strong Blade Actions
Search + Take Blade		Feint deceive (lateral)(circular)		
Counter Attack (timing)(body displacement)(opposition):				

Opponent Defense:	Parry: 2 3 4 5	Circle: 2 3 4
Sweeping parries while retreating	Counter time	2 parries

Actions that worked:	Parry riposte 2 3 4 5	Circle: 2 3 4
Pull distance – make opp fall short	Push and attack	Pull and defend
Feint deceive (4-6) (circle 3) (around 2) ( ) ( )		
Beat-disengage	False parry-real parry riposte	

Notes:

Observed on:				
Opponent:				
Who won?				
Score				

H

Name:					Country/Division:	
Club:						
Age group:	Y10	Y12	Y14	CDT	JNR OPEN	VET
Visuals:	Righty	Lefty	Taller		Shorter	Growing
Trends:	Attacker	Defender	Counter attacker			
Tactics:	Tactical	Sometimes Tactical		Not Very Tactical		
Timing:	Slow/Quick			Poor/Good Timing		
	Awkward Timing			Arrhythmic Timing		

Opponent In the Box:		Attack in Prep		Varies target	
Closeout		Beat attacks		Parry-Riposte	
Feint deceive		Counter Attack with (timing)(closeout)			
Big steps	Pull Distance (make me fall short)			Other:	
Opponent Attacks:		Simple	Composed	Long smooth attacks	
Big steps	Small steps	Beat attacks		Strong Blade Actions	
Search + Take Blade		Feint deceive (lateral)(circular)			
Counter Attack (timing)(body displacement)(opposition):					
Opponent Defense:		Parry: 2 3 4 5		Circle: 2 3 4	
Sweeping parries while retreating			Counter time		2 parries
Actions that worked:		Parry riposte 2 3 4 5		Circle: 2 3 4	
Pull distance – make opp fall short			Push and attack		Pull and defend
Feint deceive (4-6) (circle 3) (around 2) ( ) ( )					
Beat-disengage		False parry-real parry riposte			

Notes:

Observed on:					
Opponent:					
Who won?					
Score					

Name:				Country/Division:	
Club:					
Age group:	Y10	Y12	Y14	CDT	JNR	OPEN	VET
Visuals:	Righty	Lefty	Taller	Shorter	Growing
Trends:	Attacker	Defender	Counter attacker	
Tactics:	Tactical	Sometimes Tactical	Not Very Tactical	
Timing:	Slow/Quick		Poor/Good Timing	
	Awkward Timing		Arrhythmic Timing	

Opponent In the Box:	Attack in Prep	Varies target
Closeout	Beat attacks	Parry-Riposte
Feint deceive	Counter Attack with (timing)(closeout)	
Big steps	Pull Distance (make me fall short)	Other:

Opponent Attacks:		Simple	Composed	Long smooth attacks
Big steps	Small steps	Beat attacks		Strong Blade Actions
Search + Take Blade		Feint deceive (lateral)(circular)		
Counter Attack (timing)(body displacement)(opposition):				

Opponent Defense:	Parry: 2 3 4 5	Circle: 2 3 4
Sweeping parries while retreating	Counter time	2 parries

Actions that worked:	Parry riposte 2 3 4 5	Circle: 2 3 4
Pull distance – make opp fall short	Push and attack	Pull and defend
Feint deceive (4-6) (circle 3) (around 2) ( ) ( )		
Beat-disengage	False parry-real parry riposte	

Notes:

Observed on:					
Opponent:					
Who won?					
Score					

I

Name:					Country/Division:		
Club:							
Age group:	Y10	Y12	Y14	CDT	JNR	OPEN	VET
Visuals:	Righty	Lefty	Taller		Shorter		Growing
Trends:	Attacker	Defender	Counter attacker				
Tactics:	Tactical	Sometimes Tactical			Not Very Tactical		
Timing:	Slow/Quick				Poor/Good Timing		
	Awkward Timing				Arrhythmic Timing		

Opponent In the Box:		Attack in Prep		Varies target	
Closeout		Beat attacks		Parry-Riposte	
Feint deceive		Counter Attack with (timing)(closeout)			
Big steps	Pull Distance (make me fall short)			Other:	
Opponent Attacks:		Simple	Composed	Long smooth attacks	
Big steps	Small steps	Beat attacks		Strong Blade Actions	
Search + Take Blade		Feint deceive (lateral)(circular)			
Counter Attack (timing)(body displacement)(opposition):					
Opponent Defense:		Parry: 2 3 4 5		Circle: 2 3 4	
Sweeping parries while retreating		Counter time		2 parries	
Actions that worked:		Parry riposte 2 3 4 5		Circle: 2 3 4	
Pull distance – make opp fall short			Push and attack	Pull and defend	
Feint deceive (4-6) (circle 3) (around 2) (			) (	)	
Beat-disengage		False parry-real parry riposte			

Notes:

Observed on:					
Opponent:					
Who won?					
Score					

Name:						Country/Division:	
Club:							
Age group:	Y10	Y12	Y14	CDT	JNR	OPEN	VET
Visuals:	Righty	Lefty		Taller		Shorter	Growing
Trends:	Attacker	Defender		Counter attacker			
Tactics:	Tactical	Sometimes Tactical			Not Very Tactical		
Timing:	Slow/Quick				Poor/Good Timing		
	Awkward Timing				Arrhythmic Timing		

Opponent In the Box:	Attack in Prep	Varies target
Closeout	Beat attacks	Parry-Riposte
Feint deceive	Counter Attack with (timing)(closeout)	
Big steps	Pull Distance (make me fall short)	Other:

J

Opponent Attacks:	Simple	Composed	Long smooth attacks
Big steps	Small steps	Beat attacks	Strong Blade Actions
Search + Take Blade	Feint deceive (lateral)(circular)		
Counter Attack (timing)(body displacement)(opposition):			

Opponent Defense:	Parry: 2 3 4 5	Circle: 2 3 4
Sweeping parries while retreating	Counter time	2 parries

Actions that worked:	Parry riposte 2 3 4 5	Circle: 2 3 4
Pull distance – make opp fall short	Push and attack	Pull and defend
Feint deceive (4-6) (circle 3) (around 2) ( ) ( )		
Beat-disengage	False parry-real parry riposte	

Notes:

Observed on:					
Opponent:					
Who won?					
Score					

Name:					Country/Division:		
Club:							
Age group:	Y10	Y12	Y14	CDT	JNR	OPEN	VET
Visuals:	Righty	Lefty	Taller		Shorter		Growing
Trends:	Attacker	Defender	Counter attacker				
Tactics:	Tactical	Sometimes Tactical			Not Very Tactical		
Timing:	Slow/Quick			Poor/Good Timing			
	Awkward Timing			Arrhythmic Timing			

Opponent In the Box:		Attack in Prep		Varies target	
Closeout		Beat attacks		Parry-Riposte	
Feint deceive		Counter Attack with (timing)(closeout)			
Big steps		Pull Distance (make me fall short)		Other:	
Opponent Attacks:		Simple	Composed	Long smooth attacks	
Big steps	Small steps	Beat attacks		Strong Blade Actions	
Search + Take Blade		Feint deceive (lateral)(circular)			
Counter Attack (timing)(body displacement)(opposition):					
Opponent Defense:		Parry: 2 3 4 5		Circle: 2 3 4	
Sweeping parries while retreating		Counter time			2 parries
Actions that worked:		Parry riposte 2 3 4 5		Circle: 2 3 4	
Pull distance – make opp fall short			Push and attack	Pull and defend	
Feint deceive (4-6) (circle 3) (around 2) (			) (	)	
Beat-disengage		False parry-real parry riposte			

Notes:

Observed on:				
Opponent:				
Who won?				
Score				

J

Name:			Country/Division:	
Club:				
Age group:	Y10　Y12　Y14　CDT　JNR　OPEN　VET			
Visuals:	Righty	Lefty	Taller	Shorter	Growing
Trends:	Attacker	Defender	Counter attacker	
Tactics:	Tactical	Sometimes Tactical	Not Very Tactical	
Timing:	Slow/Quick		Poor/Good Timing	
	Awkward Timing		Arrhythmic Timing	

Opponent In the Box:	Attack in Prep	Varies target
Closeout	Beat attacks	Parry-Riposte
Feint deceive	Counter Attack with (timing)(closeout)	
Big steps	Pull Distance (make me fall short)	Other:

Opponent Attacks:	Simple	Composed	Long smooth attacks
Big steps	Small steps	Beat attacks	Strong Blade Actions
Search + Take Blade	Feint deceive (lateral)(circular)		
Counter Attack (timing)(body displacement)(opposition):			

Opponent Defense:	Parry: 2　3　4　5	Circle: 2　3　4	
Sweeping parries while retreating	Counter time		2 parries

Actions that worked:	Parry riposte 2 3 4 5	Circle: 2 3 4
Pull distance – make opp fall short	Push and attack	Pull and defend
Feint deceive (4-6) (circle 3) (around 2) (　　) (　　)		
Beat-disengage	False parry-real parry riposte	

Notes:

K

Observed on:				
Opponent:				
Who won?				
Score				

K

Name:		Country/Division:	
Club:			
Age group:	Y10 Y12 Y14 CDT JNR OPEN VET			
Visuals:	Righty	Lefty	Taller	Shorter	Growing
Trends:	Attacker	Defender	Counter attacker	
Tactics:	Tactical	Sometimes Tactical	Not Very Tactical	
Timing:	Slow/Quick	Poor/Good Timing		
	Awkward Timing	Arrhythmic Timing		

Opponent In the Box:	Attack in Prep	Varies target	
Closeout	Beat attacks	Parry-Riposte	
Feint deceive	Counter Attack with (timing)(closeout)		
Big steps	Pull Distance (make me fall short)	Other:	
Opponent Attacks:	Simple	Composed	Long smooth attacks
Big steps	Small steps	Beat attacks	Strong Blade Actions
Search + Take Blade	Feint deceive (lateral)(circular)		
Counter Attack (timing)(body displacement)(opposition):			
Opponent Defense:	Parry: 2 3 4 5	Circle: 2 3 4	
Sweeping parries while retreating	Counter time	2 parries	
Actions that worked:	Parry riposte 2 3 4 5	Circle: 2 3 4	
Pull distance – make opp fall short	Push and attack	Pull and defend	
Feint deceive (4-6) (circle 3) (around 2) (	) (	)	
Beat-disengage	False parry-real parry riposte		
Notes:			

Observed on:					
Opponent:					
Who won?					
Score					

Name:		Country/Division:
Club:		

Age group:	Y10	Y12	Y14	CDT	JNR	OPEN	VET
Visuals:	Righty	Lefty	Taller		Shorter		Growing
Trends:	Attacker	Defender	Counter attacker				
Tactics:	Tactical	Sometimes Tactical			Not Very Tactical		

Timing:	Slow/Quick	Poor/Good Timing
	Awkward Timing	Arrhythmic Timing

Opponent In the Box:	Attack in Prep	Varies target
Closeout	Beat attacks	Parry-Riposte
Feint deceive	Counter Attack with (timing)(closeout)	
Big steps	Pull Distance (make me fall short)	Other:

Opponent Attacks:	Simple	Composed	Long smooth attacks
Big steps	Small steps	Beat attacks	Strong Blade Actions
Search + Take Blade	Feint deceive (lateral)(circular)		
Counter Attack (timing)(body displacement)(opposition):			

K

Opponent Defense:	Parry: 2 3 4 5	Circle: 2 3 4
Sweeping parries while retreating	Counter time	2 parries

Actions that worked:	Parry riposte 2 3 4 5	Circle: 2 3 4
Pull distance – make opp fall short	Push and attack	Pull and defend
Feint deceive (4-6) (circle 3) (around 2) ( ) ( )		
Beat-disengage	False parry-real parry riposte	

Notes:					

Observed on:					
Opponent:					
Who won?					
Score					

K

Name:					Country/Division:	
Club:						
Age group:	Y10	Y12	Y14	CDT	JNR	OPEN	VET
Visuals:	Righty	Lefty	Taller	Shorter	Growing
Trends:	Attacker	Defender	Counter attacker		
Tactics:	Tactical	Sometimes Tactical	Not Very Tactical		
Timing:	Slow/Quick	Poor/Good Timing		
	Awkward Timing	Arrhythmic Timing		

Opponent In the Box:	Attack in Prep	Varies target
Closeout	Beat attacks	Parry-Riposte
Feint deceive	Counter Attack with (timing)(closeout)	
Big steps	Pull Distance (make me fall short)	Other:

Opponent Attacks:	Simple	Composed	Long smooth attacks
Big steps	Small steps	Beat attacks	Strong Blade Actions
Search + Take Blade	Feint deceive (lateral)(circular)		
Counter Attack (timing)(body displacement)(opposition):			

Opponent Defense:	Parry: 2 3 4 5	Circle: 2 3 4
Sweeping parries while retreating	Counter time	2 parries

Actions that worked:	Parry riposte 2 3 4 5	Circle: 2 3 4
Pull distance – make opp fall short	Push and attack	Pull and defend
Feint deceive (4-6) (circle 3) (around 2) ( ) ( )		
Beat-disengage	False parry-real parry riposte	

Notes:

Observed on:					
Opponent:					
Who won?					
Score					

Name:					Country/Division:		
Club:							
Age group:	Y10	Y12	Y14	CDT	JNR	OPEN	VET
Visuals:	Righty	Lefty	Taller		Shorter		Growing
Trends:	Attacker	Defender	Counter attacker				
Tactics:	Tactical	Sometimes Tactical			Not Very Tactical		
Timing:	Slow/Quick			Poor/Good Timing			
	Awkward Timing			Arrhythmic Timing			

Opponent In the Box:	Attack in Prep		Varies target	
Closeout	Beat attacks		Parry-Riposte	
Feint deceive	Counter Attack with (timing)(closeout)			
Big steps	Pull Distance (make me fall short)		Other:	
Opponent Attacks:	Simple	Composed	Long smooth attacks	
Big steps	Small steps	Beat attacks	Strong Blade Actions	
Search + Take Blade	Feint deceive (lateral)(circular)			
Counter Attack (timing)(body displacement)(opposition):				
Opponent Defense:	Parry: 2 3 4 5		Circle: 2 3 4	
Sweeping parries while retreating		Counter time		2 parries
Actions that worked:	Parry riposte 2 3 4 5		Circle: 2 3 4	
Pull distance – make opp fall short		Push and attack	Pull and defend	
Feint deceive (4-6) (circle 3) (around 2) (		) (	)	
Beat-disengage	False parry-real parry riposte			

K

Notes:

Observed on:				
Opponent:				
Who won?				
Score				

K

Name:		Country/Division:	
Club:			

Age group:	Y10	Y12	Y14	CDT	JNR	OPEN	VET
Visuals:	Righty	Lefty		Taller		Shorter	Growing
Trends:	Attacker	Defender		Counter attacker			
Tactics:	Tactical	Sometimes Tactical			Not Very Tactical		
Timing:	Slow/Quick			Poor/Good Timing			
	Awkward Timing			Arrhythmic Timing			

Opponent In the Box:		Attack in Prep		Varies target	
Closeout		Beat attacks		Parry-Riposte	
Feint deceive		Counter Attack with (timing)(closeout)			
Big steps		Pull Distance (make me fall short)		Other:	
Opponent Attacks:		Simple	Composed	Long smooth attacks	
Big steps	Small steps	Beat attacks		Strong Blade Actions	
Search + Take Blade		Feint deceive (lateral)(circular)			
Counter Attack (timing)(body displacement)(opposition):					
Opponent Defense:		Parry: 2 3 4 5		Circle: 2 3 4	
Sweeping parries while retreating		Counter time		2 parries	
Actions that worked:		Parry riposte 2 3 4 5		Circle: 2 3 4	
Pull distance – make opp fall short		Push and attack		Pull and defend	
Feint deceive (4-6) (circle 3) (around 2) ( ) ( )					
Beat-disengage		False parry-real parry riposte			

Notes:	

Observed on:					
Opponent:					
Who won?					
Score					

Name:					Country/Division:	
Club:						
Age group:	Y10	Y12	Y14	CDT	JNR	OPEN	VET
Visuals:	Righty	Lefty	Taller	Shorter	Growing
Trends:	Attacker	Defender	Counter attacker	
Tactics:	Tactical	Sometimes Tactical	Not Very Tactical
Timing:	Slow/Quick	Poor/Good Timing
	Awkward Timing	Arrhythmic Timing

Opponent In the Box:	Attack in Prep	Varies target
Closeout	Beat attacks	Parry-Riposte
Feint deceive	Counter Attack with (timing)(closeout)	
Big steps	Pull Distance (make me fall short)	Other:

Opponent Attacks:	Simple	Composed	Long smooth attacks
Big steps	Small steps	Beat attacks	Strong Blade Actions
Search + Take Blade	Feint deceive (lateral)(circular)	
Counter Attack (timing)(body displacement)(opposition):			

L

Opponent Defense:	Parry: 2 3 4 5	Circle: 2 3 4
Sweeping parries while retreating	Counter time	2 parries

Actions that worked:	Parry riposte 2 3 4 5	Circle: 2 3 4
Pull distance – make opp fall short	Push and attack	Pull and defend
Feint deceive (4-6) (circle 3) (around 2) ( ) ( )		
Beat-disengage	False parry-real parry riposte	

Notes:

Observed on:				
Opponent:				
Who won?				
Score				

Name:					Country/Division:	
Club:						
Age group:	Y10	Y12	Y14	CDT	JNR	OPEN	VET
Visuals:	Righty	Lefty	Taller		Shorter	Growing
Trends:	Attacker	Defender	Counter attacker			
Tactics:	Tactical	Sometimes Tactical		Not Very Tactical		
Timing:	Slow/Quick			Poor/Good Timing		
	Awkward Timing			Arrhythmic Timing		

L

Opponent In the Box:	Attack in Prep	Varies target
Closeout	Beat attacks	Parry-Riposte
Feint deceive	Counter Attack with (timing)(closeout)	
Big steps	Pull Distance (make me fall short)	Other:

Opponent Attacks:	Simple	Composed	Long smooth attacks
Big steps	Small steps	Beat attacks	Strong Blade Actions
Search + Take Blade	Feint deceive (lateral)(circular)		
Counter Attack (timing)(body displacement)(opposition):			

Opponent Defense:	Parry: 2 3 4 5	Circle: 2 3 4
Sweeping parries while retreating	Counter time	2 parries

Actions that worked:	Parry riposte 2 3 4 5	Circle: 2 3 4
Pull distance – make opp fall short	Push and attack	Pull and defend
Feint deceive (4-6) (circle 3) (around 2) ( ) ( )		
Beat-disengage	False parry-real parry riposte	

Notes:	

Observed on:					
Opponent:					
Who won?					
Score					

Name:				Country/Division:	
Club:					
Age group:	Y10	Y12	Y14	CDT	JNR	OPEN	VET
Visuals:	Righty	Lefty	Taller	Shorter	Growing
Trends:	Attacker	Defender	Counter attacker		
Tactics:	Tactical	Sometimes Tactical		Not Very Tactical	
Timing:	Slow/Quick		Poor/Good Timing		
	Awkward Timing		Arrhythmic Timing		

Opponent In the Box:	Attack in Prep	Varies target
Closeout	Beat attacks	Parry-Riposte
Feint deceive	Counter Attack with (timing)(closeout)	
Big steps	Pull Distance (make me fall short)	Other:

Opponent Attacks:		Simple	Composed	Long smooth attacks
Big steps	Small steps	Beat attacks		Strong Blade Actions
Search + Take Blade		Feint deceive (lateral)(circular)		
Counter Attack (timing)(body displacement)(opposition):				

L

Opponent Defense:	Parry: 2 3 4 5	Circle: 2 3 4	
Sweeping parries while retreating	Counter time		2 parries

Actions that worked:	Parry riposte 2 3 4 5	Circle: 2 3 4
Pull distance – make opp fall short	Push and attack	Pull and defend
Feint deceive (4-6) (circle 3) (around 2) ( ) ( )		
Beat-disengage	False parry-real parry riposte	

Notes:	

Observed on:				
Opponent:				
Who won?				
Score				

Name:					Country/Division:	
Club:						
Age group:	Y10	Y12	Y14	CDT	JNR	OPEN	VET
Visuals:	Righty	Lefty	Taller		Shorter	Growing
Trends:	Attacker	Defender	Counter attacker			
Tactics:	Tactical	Sometimes Tactical		Not Very Tactical		
Timing:	Slow/Quick			Poor/Good Timing		
	Awkward Timing			Arrhythmic Timing		
Opponent In the Box:	Attack in Prep			Varies target		
Closeout	Beat attacks			Parry-Riposte		
Feint deceive	Counter Attack with (timing)(closeout)					
Big steps	Pull Distance (make me fall short)			Other:		
Opponent Attacks:	Simple		Composed	Long smooth attacks		
Big steps	Small steps	Beat attacks		Strong Blade Actions		
Search + Take Blade	Feint deceive (lateral)(circular)					
Counter Attack (timing)(body displacement)(opposition):						
Opponent Defense:	Parry: 2 3 4 5			Circle: 2 3 4		
Sweeping parries while retreating		Counter time			2 parries	
Actions that worked:	Parry riposte 2 3 4 5			Circle: 2 3 4		
Pull distance – make opp fall short			Push and attack		Pull and defend	
Feint deceive (4-6) (circle 3) (around 2) ( ) ( )						
Beat-disengage	False parry-real parry riposte					
Notes:						

L

Observed on:					
Opponent:					
Who won?					
Score					

Name:					Country/Division:	
Club:						
Age group:	Y10	Y12	Y14	CDT	JNR	OPEN	VET
Visuals:	Righty	Lefty	Taller	Shorter	Growing
Trends:	Attacker	Defender	Counter attacker	
Tactics:	Tactical	Sometimes Tactical	Not Very Tactical	
Timing:	Slow/Quick		Poor/Good Timing	
	Awkward Timing		Arrhythmic Timing	

Opponent In the Box:	Attack in Prep	Varies target
Closeout	Beat attacks	Parry-Riposte
Feint deceive	Counter Attack with (timing)(closeout)	
Big steps	Pull Distance (make me fall short)	Other:

Opponent Attacks:		Simple	Composed	Long smooth attacks
Big steps	Small steps	Beat attacks		Strong Blade Actions
Search + Take Blade	Feint deceive (lateral)(circular)			
Counter Attack (timing)(body displacement)(opposition):				

L

Opponent Defense:	Parry: 2 3 4 5	Circle: 2 3 4	
Sweeping parries while retreating	Counter time		2 parries

Actions that worked:	Parry riposte 2 3 4 5	Circle: 2 3 4
Pull distance – make opp fall short	Push and attack	Pull and defend
Feint deceive (4-6) (circle 3) (around 2) ( ) ( )		
Beat-disengage	False parry-real parry riposte	

Notes:	

Observed on:					
Opponent:					
Who won?					
Score					

Name:					Country/Division:		
Club:							
Age group:	Y10	Y12	Y14	CDT	JNR	OPEN	VET
Visuals:	Righty	Lefty	Taller		Shorter		Growing
Trends:	Attacker	Defender	Counter attacker				
Tactics:	Tactical	Sometimes Tactical			Not Very Tactical		
Timing:	Slow/Quick				Poor/Good Timing		
	Awkward Timing				Arrhythmic Timing		

L

Opponent In the Box:		Attack in Prep		Varies target	
Closeout		Beat attacks		Parry-Riposte	
Feint deceive		Counter Attack with (timing)(closeout)			
Big steps		Pull Distance (make me fall short)		Other:	
Opponent Attacks:		Simple	Composed	Long smooth attacks	
Big steps	Small steps	Beat attacks		Strong Blade Actions	
Search + Take Blade		Feint deceive (lateral)(circular)			
Counter Attack (timing)(body displacement)(opposition):					
Opponent Defense:		Parry: 2 3 4 5		Circle: 2 3 4	
Sweeping parries while retreating			Counter time		2 parries
Actions that worked:		Parry riposte 2 3 4 5		Circle: 2 3 4	
Pull distance – make opp fall short			Push and attack		Pull and defend
Feint deceive (4-6) (circle 3) (around 2) ( ) ( )					
Beat-disengage		False parry-real parry riposte			
Notes:					
Observed on:					
Opponent:					
Who won?					
Score					

Name:				Country/Division:	
Club:					
Age group:	Y10	Y12	Y14	CDT	JNR	OPEN	VET
Visuals:	Righty	Lefty	Taller	Shorter	Growing
Trends:	Attacker	Defender	Counter attacker	
Tactics:	Tactical	Sometimes Tactical	Not Very Tactical
Timing:	Slow/Quick		Poor/Good Timing	
	Awkward Timing		Arrhythmic Timing	

Opponent In the Box:	Attack in Prep	Varies target
Closeout	Beat attacks	Parry-Riposte
Feint deceive	Counter Attack with (timing)(closeout)	
Big steps	Pull Distance (make me fall short)	Other:

Opponent Attacks:		Simple	Composed	Long smooth attacks
Big steps	Small steps	Beat attacks		Strong Blade Actions
Search + Take Blade	Feint deceive (lateral)(circular)			
Counter Attack (timing)(body displacement)(opposition):				

Opponent Defense:	Parry: 2 3 4 5	Circle: 2 3 4
Sweeping parries while retreating	Counter time	2 parries

Actions that worked:	Parry riposte 2 3 4 5	Circle: 2 3 4
Pull distance – make opp fall short	Push and attack	Pull and defend
Feint deceive (4-6) (circle 3) (around 2) ( ) ( )		
Beat-disengage	False parry-real parry riposte	

Notes:

M

Observed on:					
Opponent:					
Who won?					
Score					

Name:					Country/Division:	
Club:						
Age group:	Y10	Y12	Y14	CDT	JNR	OPEN	VET
Visuals:	Righty	Lefty	Taller		Shorter	Growing
Trends:	Attacker	Defender	Counter attacker			
Tactics:	Tactical	Sometimes Tactical		Not Very Tactical		
Timing:	Slow/Quick		Poor/Good Timing			
	Awkward Timing		Arrhythmic Timing			

Opponent In the Box:	Attack in Prep	Varies target
Closeout	Beat attacks	Parry-Riposte
Feint deceive	Counter Attack with (timing)(closeout)	
Big steps	Pull Distance (make me fall short)	Other:

Opponent Attacks:		Simple	Composed	Long smooth attacks
Big steps	Small steps	Beat attacks		Strong Blade Actions
Search + Take Blade		Feint deceive (lateral)(circular)		
Counter Attack (timing)(body displacement)(opposition):				

Opponent Defense:	Parry: 2 3 4 5	Circle: 2 3 4
Sweeping parries while retreating	Counter time	2 parries

Actions that worked:	Parry riposte 2 3 4 5	Circle: 2 3 4
Pull distance – make opp fall short	Push and attack	Pull and defend
Feint deceive (4-6) (circle 3) (around 2) ( ) ( )		
Beat-disengage	False parry-real parry riposte	

Notes:

Observed on:				
Opponent:				
Who won?				
Score				

M

Name:				Country/Division:	
Club:					
Age group:	Y10	Y12 Y14	CDT	JNR OPEN	VET
Visuals:	Righty	Lefty	Taller	Shorter	Growing
Trends:	Attacker	Defender	Counter attacker		
Tactics:	Tactical	Sometimes Tactical		Not Very Tactical	
Timing:	Slow/Quick		Poor/Good Timing		
	Awkward Timing		Arrhythmic Timing		

Opponent In the Box:	Attack in Prep	Varies target
Closeout	Beat attacks	Parry-Riposte
Feint deceive	Counter Attack with (timing)(closeout)	
Big steps	Pull Distance (make me fall short)	Other:

Opponent Attacks:		Simple	Composed	Long smooth attacks
Big steps	Small steps	Beat attacks		Strong Blade Actions
Search + Take Blade		Feint deceive (lateral)(circular)		
Counter Attack (timing)(body displacement)(opposition):				

Opponent Defense:	Parry: 2 3 4 5		Circle: 2 3 4	
Sweeping parries while retreating		Counter time		2 parries

Actions that worked:	Parry riposte 2 3 4 5	Circle: 2 3 4	
Pull distance – make opp fall short		Push and attack	Pull and defend
Feint deceive (4-6) (circle 3) (around 2) ( ) ( )			
Beat-disengage	False parry-real parry riposte		

M

Notes:				

Observed on:				
Opponent:				
Who won?				
Score				

Name:					Country/Division:	
Club:						
Age group:	Y10	Y12	Y14	CDT	JNR	OPEN	VET
Visuals:	Righty	Lefty	Taller		Shorter	Growing
Trends:	Attacker	Defender	Counter attacker			
Tactics:	Tactical	Sometimes Tactical		Not Very Tactical		
Timing:	Slow/Quick		Poor/Good Timing			
	Awkward Timing		Arrhythmic Timing			
Opponent In the Box:		Attack in Prep		Varies target		
Closeout		Beat attacks		Parry-Riposte		
Feint deceive		Counter Attack with (timing)(closeout)		Other:		
Big steps	Pull Distance (make me fall short)					
Opponent Attacks:		Simple	Composed	Long smooth attacks		
Big steps	Small steps	Beat attacks		Strong Blade Actions		
Search + Take Blade		Feint deceive (lateral)(circular)				
Counter Attack (timing)(body displacement)(opposition):						
Opponent Defense:		Parry: 2 3 4 5		Circle: 2 3 4		
Sweeping parries while retreating		Counter time		2 parries		
Actions that worked:		Parry riposte 2 3 4 5		Circle: 2 3 4		
Pull distance – make opp fall short			Push and attack	Pull and defend		
Feint deceive (4-6) (circle 3) (around 2) ( ) ( )						
Beat-disengage		False parry-real parry riposte				
Notes:						
Observed on:						
Opponent:						
Who won?						
Score						

M

Name:				Country/Division:	
Club:					
Age group:	Y10	Y12	Y14	CDT	JNR	OPEN	VET
Visuals:	Righty	Lefty	Taller	Shorter	Growing
Trends:	Attacker	Defender	Counter attacker	
Tactics:	Tactical	Sometimes Tactical	Not Very Tactical
Timing:	Slow/Quick		Poor/Good Timing	
	Awkward Timing		Arrhythmic Timing	

Opponent In the Box:	Attack in Prep	Varies target
Closeout	Beat attacks	Parry-Riposte
Feint deceive	Counter Attack with (timing)(closeout)
Big steps	Pull Distance (make me fall short)	Other:

Opponent Attacks:	Simple	Composed	Long smooth attacks
Big steps	Small steps	Beat attacks	Strong Blade Actions
Search + Take Blade	Feint deceive (lateral)(circular)
Counter Attack (timing)(body displacement)(opposition):

Opponent Defense:	Parry: 2 3 4 5	Circle: 2 3 4
Sweeping parries while retreating	Counter time	2 parries

Actions that worked:	Parry riposte 2 3 4 5	Circle: 2 3 4
Pull distance – make opp fall short	Push and attack	Pull and defend
Feint deceive (4-6) (circle 3) (around 2) (   ) (   )
Beat-disengage	False parry-real parry riposte

Notes:

M

Observed on:				
Opponent:				
Who won?				
Score				

Name:					Country/Division:	
Club:						
Age group:	Y10	Y12	Y14	CDT	JNR OPEN	VET
Visuals:	Righty	Lefty		Taller	Shorter	Growing
Trends:	Attacker	Defender		Counter attacker		
Tactics:	Tactical	Sometimes Tactical			Not Very Tactical	
Timing:	Slow/Quick			Poor/Good Timing		
	Awkward Timing			Arrhythmic Timing		

Opponent In the Box:	Attack in Prep	Varies target
Closeout	Beat attacks	Parry-Riposte
Feint deceive	Counter Attack with (timing)(closeout)	
Big steps	Pull Distance (make me fall short)	Other:

Opponent Attacks:		Simple	Composed	Long smooth attacks
Big steps	Small steps	Beat attacks		Strong Blade Actions
Search + Take Blade		Feint deceive (lateral)(circular)		
Counter Attack (timing)(body displacement)(opposition):				

M

Opponent Defense:	Parry: 2 3 4 5	Circle: 2 3 4	
Sweeping parries while retreating	Counter time		2 parries

Actions that worked:	Parry riposte 2 3 4 5	Circle: 2 3 4	
Pull distance – make opp fall short		Push and attack	Pull and defend
Feint deceive (4-6) (circle 3) (around 2) (	) (	)	
Beat-disengage	False parry-real parry riposte		

Notes:	

Observed on:					
Opponent:					
Who won?					
Score					

Name:						Country/Division:	
Club:							
Age group:	Y10	Y12	Y14	CDT	JNR	OPEN	VET
Visuals:	Righty	Lefty	Taller		Shorter	Growing	
Trends:	Attacker	Defender	Counter attacker				
Tactics:	Tactical	Sometimes Tactical			Not Very Tactical		
Timing:	Slow/Quick			Poor/Good Timing			
	Awkward Timing			Arrhythmic Timing			

Opponent In the Box:	Attack in Prep	Varies target
Closeout	Beat attacks	Parry-Riposte
Feint deceive	Counter Attack with (timing)(closeout)	
Big steps	Pull Distance (make me fall short)	Other:

Opponent Attacks:	Simple	Composed	Long smooth attacks
Big steps	Small steps	Beat attacks	Strong Blade Actions
Search + Take Blade	Feint deceive (lateral)(circular)		
Counter Attack (timing)(body displacement)(opposition):			

Opponent Defense:	Parry: 2 3 4 5	Circle: 2 3 4
Sweeping parries while retreating	Counter time	2 parries

Actions that worked:	Parry riposte 2 3 4 5	Circle: 2 3 4
Pull distance – make opp fall short	Push and attack	Pull and defend
Feint deceive (4-6) (circle 3) (around 2) ( ) ( )		
Beat-disengage	False parry-real parry riposte	

Notes:

M

Observed on:				
Opponent:				
Who won?				
Score				

Name:					Country/Division:	
Club:						
Age group:	Y10	Y12	Y14	CDT	JNR	OPEN	VET
Visuals:	Righty	Lefty	Taller		Shorter	Growing
Trends:	Attacker	Defender	Counter attacker			
Tactics:	Tactical	Sometimes Tactical		Not Very Tactical		
Timing:	Slow/Quick		Poor/Good Timing			
	Awkward Timing		Arrhythmic Timing			

Opponent In the Box:		Attack in Prep	Varies target	
Closeout		Beat attacks	Parry-Riposte	
Feint deceive		Counter Attack with (timing)(closeout)		
Big steps	Pull Distance (make me fall short)		Other:	
Opponent Attacks:		Simple	Composed	Long smooth attacks
Big steps	Small steps	Beat attacks		Strong Blade Actions
Search + Take Blade		Feint deceive (lateral)(circular)		
Counter Attack (timing)(body displacement)(opposition):				
Opponent Defense:		Parry: 2 3 4 5	Circle: 2 3 4	
Sweeping parries while retreating		Counter time		2 parries
Actions that worked:		Parry riposte 2 3 4 5	Circle: 2 3 4	
Pull distance – make opp fall short			Push and attack	Pull and defend
Feint deceive (4-6) (circle 3) (around 2) ( ) ( )				
Beat-disengage		False parry-real parry riposte		
Notes:				

M

Observed on:					
Opponent:					
Who won?					
Score					

Name:				Country/Division:	
Club:					
Age group:	Y10	Y12	Y14	CDT	JNR	OPEN	VET
Visuals:	Righty	Lefty	Taller	Shorter	Growing
Trends:	Attacker	Defender	Counter attacker	
Tactics:	Tactical	Sometimes Tactical	Not Very Tactical	
Timing:	Slow/Quick		Poor/Good Timing	
	Awkward Timing		Arrhythmic Timing	

Opponent In the Box:	Attack in Prep	Varies target
Closeout	Beat attacks	Parry-Riposte
Feint deceive	Counter Attack with (timing)(closeout)	
Big steps	Pull Distance (make me fall short)	Other:

Opponent Attacks:	Simple	Composed	Long smooth attacks
Big steps	Small steps	Beat attacks	Strong Blade Actions
Search + Take Blade	Feint deceive (lateral)(circular)		
Counter Attack (timing)(body displacement)(opposition):			

Opponent Defense:	Parry: 2 3 4 5	Circle: 2 3 4
Sweeping parries while retreating	Counter time	2 parries

Actions that worked:	Parry riposte 2 3 4 5	Circle: 2 3 4
Pull distance – make opp fall short	Push and attack	Pull and defend
Feint deceive (4-6) (circle 3) (around 2) ( ) ( )		
Beat-disengage	False parry-real parry riposte	

Notes:

Observed on:					
Opponent:					
Who won?					
Score					

N

Name:					Country/Division:	
Club:						
Age group:	Y10	Y12	Y14	CDT	JNR	OPEN	VET
Visuals:	Righty	Lefty	Taller		Shorter	Growing
Trends:	Attacker	Defender	Counter attacker			
Tactics:	Tactical	Sometimes Tactical		Not Very Tactical		
Timing:	Slow/Quick		Poor/Good Timing			
	Awkward Timing		Arrhythmic Timing			

Opponent In the Box:		Attack in Prep		Varies target	
Closeout		Beat attacks		Parry-Riposte	
Feint deceive		Counter Attack with (timing)(closeout)			
Big steps		Pull Distance (make me fall short)		Other:	
Opponent Attacks:		Simple	Composed	Long smooth attacks	
Big steps	Small steps	Beat attacks		Strong Blade Actions	
Search + Take Blade		Feint deceive (lateral)(circular)			
Counter Attack (timing)(body displacement)(opposition):					
Opponent Defense:		Parry: 2 3 4 5		Circle: 2 3 4	
Sweeping parries while retreating			Counter time		2 parries
Actions that worked:		Parry riposte 2 3 4 5		Circle: 2 3 4	
Pull distance – make opp fall short			Push and attack		Pull and defend
Feint deceive (4-6) (circle 3) (around 2) ( ) ( )					
Beat-disengage		False parry-real parry riposte			
Notes:					
Observed on:					
Opponent:					
Who won?					
Score					

Name:					Country/Division:	
Club:						
Age group:	Y10	Y12	Y14	CDT	JNR OPEN	VET
Visuals:	Righty	Lefty	Taller		Shorter	Growing
Trends:	Attacker	Defender	Counter attacker			
Tactics:	Tactical	Sometimes Tactical			Not Very Tactical	
Timing:	Slow/Quick			Poor/Good Timing		
	Awkward Timing			Arrhythmic Timing		

Opponent In the Box:	Attack in Prep	Varies target
Closeout	Beat attacks	Parry-Riposte
Feint deceive	Counter Attack with (timing)(closeout)	
Big steps	Pull Distance (make me fall short)	Other:

Opponent Attacks:		Simple	Composed	Long smooth attacks
Big steps	Small steps	Beat attacks		Strong Blade Actions
Search + Take Blade		Feint deceive (lateral)(circular)		
Counter Attack (timing)(body displacement)(opposition):				

Opponent Defense:	Parry: 2 3 4 5	Circle: 2 3 4
Sweeping parries while retreating	Counter time	2 parries

Actions that worked:	Parry riposte 2 3 4 5	Circle: 2 3 4
Pull distance – make opp fall short	Push and attack	Pull and defend
Feint deceive (4-6) (circle 3) (around 2) ( ) ( )		
Beat-disengage	False parry-real parry riposte	

Notes:

Observed on:				
Opponent:				
Who won?				
Score				

N

Name:					Country/Division:	
Club:						
Age group:	Y10	Y12	Y14	CDT	JNR	OPEN	VET
Visuals:	Righty	Lefty	Taller		Shorter	Growing
Trends:	Attacker	Defender	Counter attacker			
Tactics:	Tactical	Sometimes Tactical		Not Very Tactical		
Timing:	Slow/Quick		Poor/Good Timing			
	Awkward Timing		Arrhythmic Timing			

Opponent In the Box:	Attack in Prep		Varies target	
Closeout		Beat attacks		Parry-Riposte
Feint deceive		Counter Attack with (timing)(closeout)		
Big steps	Pull Distance (make me fall short)		Other:	
Opponent Attacks:		Simple	Composed	Long smooth attacks
Big steps	Small steps	Beat attacks		Strong Blade Actions
Search + Take Blade		Feint deceive (lateral)(circular)		
Counter Attack (timing)(body displacement)(opposition):				
Opponent Defense:		Parry: 2 3 4 5	Circle: 2 3 4	
Sweeping parries while retreating		Counter time		2 parries
Actions that worked:		Parry riposte 2 3 4 5	Circle: 2 3 4	
Pull distance – make opp fall short			Push and attack	Pull and defend
Feint deceive (4-6) (circle 3) (around 2) ( ) ( )				
Beat-disengage		False parry-real parry riposte		

Notes:

Observed on:					
Opponent:					
Who won?					
Score					

N

Name:				Country/Division:	
Club:					
Age group:	Y10 Y12 Y14		CDT JNR	OPEN VET	
Visuals:	Righty	Lefty	Taller	Shorter	Growing
Trends:	Attacker	Defender	Counter attacker		
Tactics:	Tactical	Sometimes Tactical		Not Very Tactical	
Timing:	Slow/Quick		Poor/Good Timing		
	Awkward Timing		Arrhythmic Timing		

Opponent In the Box:		Attack in Prep		Varies target	
Closeout		Beat attacks		Parry-Riposte	
Feint deceive		Counter Attack with (timing)(closeout)			
Big steps	Pull Distance (make me fall short)			Other:	

Opponent Attacks:		Simple	Composed	Long smooth attacks
Big steps	Small steps	Beat attacks		Strong Blade Actions
Search + Take Blade		Feint deceive (lateral)(circular)		
Counter Attack (timing)(body displacement)(opposition):				

Opponent Defense:	Parry: 2 3 4 5		Circle: 2 3 4	
Sweeping parries while retreating		Counter time		2 parries

Actions that worked:	Parry riposte 2 3 4 5		Circle: 2 3 4	
Pull distance – make opp fall short		Push and attack		Pull and defend
Feint deceive (4-6) (circle 3) (around 2) ( ) ( )				
Beat-disengage	False parry-real parry riposte			

Notes:

Observed on:					
Opponent:					
Who won?					
Score					

O

Name:					Country/Division:	
Club:						
Age group:	Y10	Y12	Y14	CDT	JNR OPEN	VET
Visuals:	Righty	Lefty	Taller		Shorter	Growing
Trends:	Attacker	Defender	Counter attacker			
Tactics:	Tactical	Sometimes Tactical			Not Very Tactical	
Timing:	Slow/Quick			Poor/Good Timing		
	Awkward Timing			Arrhythmic Timing		

Opponent In the Box:	Attack in Prep	Varies target	
Closeout	Beat attacks	Parry-Riposte	
Feint deceive	Counter Attack with (timing)(closeout)		
Big steps	Pull Distance (make me fall short)	Other:	
Opponent Attacks:	Simple	Composed	Long smooth attacks
Big steps	Small steps	Beat attacks	Strong Blade Actions
Search + Take Blade	Feint deceive (lateral)(circular)		
Counter Attack (timing)(body displacement)(opposition):			
Opponent Defense:	Parry: 2 3 4 5	Circle: 2 3 4	
Sweeping parries while retreating	Counter time		2 parries
Actions that worked:	Parry riposte 2 3 4 5	Circle: 2 3 4	
Pull distance – make opp fall short	Push and attack	Pull and defend	
Feint deceive (4-6) (circle 3) (around 2) ( ) ( )			
Beat-disengage	False parry-real parry riposte		
Notes:			

Observed on:					
Opponent:					
Who won?					
Score					

Name:						Country/Division:	
Club:							
Age group:	Y10	Y12	Y14	CDT	JNR	OPEN	VET
Visuals:	Righty	Lefty		Taller		Shorter	Growing
Trends:	Attacker	Defender		Counter attacker			
Tactics:	Tactical	Sometimes Tactical				Not Very Tactical	
Timing:	Slow/Quick				Poor/Good Timing		
	Awkward Timing				Arrhythmic Timing		

Opponent In the Box:	Attack in Prep		Varies target	
Closeout	Beat attacks		Parry-Riposte	
Feint deceive	Counter Attack with (timing)(closeout)			
Big steps	Pull Distance (make me fall short)		Other:	
Opponent Attacks:	Simple	Composed	Long smooth attacks	
Big steps	Small steps	Beat attacks	Strong Blade Actions	
Search + Take Blade	Feint deceive (lateral)(circular)			
Counter Attack (timing)(body displacement)(opposition):				
Opponent Defense:	Parry: 2 3 4 5		Circle: 2 3 4	
Sweeping parries while retreating	Counter time		2 parries	
Actions that worked:	Parry riposte 2 3 4 5		Circle: 2 3 4	
Pull distance – make opp fall short	Push and attack		Pull and defend	
Feint deceive (4-6) (circle 3) (around 2) ( ) ( )				
Beat-disengage	False parry-real parry riposte			

P

Notes:

Observed on:				
Opponent:				
Who won?				
Score				

Name:					Country/Division:	
Club:						
Age group:	Y10	Y12	Y14	CDT	JNR	OPEN	VET
Visuals:	Righty	Lefty	Taller	Shorter	Growing
Trends:	Attacker	Defender	Counter attacker		
Tactics:	Tactical	Sometimes Tactical	Not Very Tactical		
Timing:	Slow/Quick		Poor/Good Timing		
	Awkward Timing		Arrhythmic Timing		

Opponent In the Box:	Attack in Prep	Varies target
Closeout	Beat attacks	Parry-Riposte
Feint deceive	Counter Attack with (timing)(closeout)	
Big steps	Pull Distance (make me fall short)	Other:

Opponent Attacks:	Simple	Composed	Long smooth attacks
Big steps	Small steps	Beat attacks	Strong Blade Actions
Search + Take Blade	Feint deceive (lateral)(circular)		
Counter Attack (timing)(body displacement)(opposition):			

Opponent Defense:	Parry: 2 3 4 5	Circle: 2 3 4
Sweeping parries while retreating	Counter time	2 parries

Actions that worked:	Parry riposte 2 3 4 5	Circle: 2 3 4
Pull distance – make opp fall short	Push and attack	Pull and defend
Feint deceive (4-6) (circle 3) (around 2) ( ) ( )		
Beat-disengage	False parry-real parry riposte	

Notes:

P

Observed on:				
Opponent:				
Who won?				
Score				

Name:						Country/Division:	
Club:							
Age group:	Y10	Y12	Y14	CDT	JNR	OPEN	VET
Visuals:	Righty	Lefty		Taller	Shorter		Growing
Trends:	Attacker	Defender		Counter attacker			
Tactics:	Tactical	Sometimes Tactical			Not Very Tactical		
Timing:	Slow/Quick				Poor/Good Timing		
	Awkward Timing				Arrhythmic Timing		

Opponent In the Box:	Attack in Prep		Varies target	
Closeout	Beat attacks		Parry-Riposte	
Feint deceive	Counter Attack with (timing)(closeout)			
Big steps	Pull Distance (make me fall short)		Other:	
Opponent Attacks:	Simple	Composed	Long smooth attacks	
Big steps	Small steps	Beat attacks	Strong Blade Actions	
Search + Take Blade	Feint deceive (lateral)(circular)			
Counter Attack (timing)(body displacement)(opposition):				
Opponent Defense:	Parry: 2 3 4 5		Circle: 2 3 4	
Sweeping parries while retreating		Counter time		2 parries
Actions that worked:	Parry riposte 2 3 4 5		Circle: 2 3 4	
Pull distance – make opp fall short		Push and attack	Pull and defend	
Feint deceive (4-6) (circle 3) (around 2) ( ) ( )				
Beat-disengage	False parry-real parry riposte			

P

Notes:				
Observed on:				
Opponent:				
Who won?				
Score				

Name:					Country/Division:		
Club:							
Age group:	Y10	Y12	Y14	CDT	JNR	OPEN	VET
Visuals:	Righty	Lefty		Taller		Shorter	Growing
Trends:	Attacker	Defender		Counter attacker			
Tactics:	Tactical	Sometimes Tactical			Not Very Tactical		
Timing:	Slow/Quick				Poor/Good Timing		
	Awkward Timing				Arrhythmic Timing		

Opponent In the Box:		Attack in Prep		Varies target	
Closeout		Beat attacks		Parry-Riposte	
Feint deceive		Counter Attack with (timing)(closeout)			
Big steps		Pull Distance (make me fall short)		Other:	
Opponent Attacks:		Simple	Composed	Long smooth attacks	
Big steps	Small steps	Beat attacks		Strong Blade Actions	
Search + Take Blade		Feint deceive (lateral)(circular)			
Counter Attack (timing)(body displacement)(opposition):					
Opponent Defense:		Parry: 2 3 4 5		Circle: 2 3 4	
Sweeping parries while retreating		Counter time			2 parries
Actions that worked:		Parry riposte 2 3 4 5		Circle: 2 3 4	
Pull distance – make opp fall short		Push and attack		Pull and defend	
Feint deceive (4-6) (circle 3) (around 2) ( ) ( )					
Beat-disengage		False parry-real parry riposte			
Notes:					

P

Observed on:					
Opponent:					
Who won?					
Score					

Name:				Country/Division:	
Club:					
Age group:	Y10	Y12 Y14	CDT	JNR OPEN	VET
Visuals:	Righty	Lefty	Taller	Shorter	Growing
Trends:	Attacker	Defender	Counter attacker		
Tactics:	Tactical	Sometimes Tactical		Not Very Tactical	
Timing:	Slow/Quick		Poor/Good Timing		
	Awkward Timing		Arrhythmic Timing		

Opponent In the Box:		Attack in Prep		Varies target	
Closeout		Beat attacks		Parry-Riposte	
Feint deceive		Counter Attack with (timing)(closeout)			
Big steps	Pull Distance (make me fall short)			Other:	
Opponent Attacks:		Simple	Composed	Long smooth attacks	
Big steps	Small steps	Beat attacks		Strong Blade Actions	
Search + Take Blade		Feint deceive (lateral)(circular)			
Counter Attack (timing)(body displacement)(opposition):					
Opponent Defense:		Parry: 2 3 4 5		Circle: 2 3 4	
Sweeping parries while retreating		Counter time		2 parries	
Actions that worked:		Parry riposte 2 3 4 5		Circle: 2 3 4	
Pull distance – make opp fall short			Push and attack	Pull and defend	
Feint deceive (4-6) (circle 3) (around 2) ( ) ( )					
Beat-disengage		False parry-real parry riposte			
Notes:					
Observed on:					
Opponent:					
Who won?					
Score					

P

Name:					Country/Division:		
Club:							
Age group:	Y10	Y12	Y14	CDT	JNR	OPEN	VET
Visuals:	Righty	Lefty	Taller		Shorter		Growing
Trends:	Attacker	Defender	Counter attacker				
Tactics:	Tactical	Sometimes Tactical			Not Very Tactical		
Timing:	Slow/Quick				Poor/Good Timing		
	Awkward Timing				Arrhythmic Timing		

Opponent In the Box:		Attack in Prep		Varies target	
Closeout		Beat attacks		Parry-Riposte	
Feint deceive		Counter Attack with (timing)(closeout)			
Big steps	Pull Distance (make me fall short)			Other:	
Opponent Attacks:		Simple	Composed	Long smooth attacks	
Big steps	Small steps	Beat attacks		Strong Blade Actions	
Search + Take Blade		Feint deceive (lateral)(circular)			
Counter Attack (timing)(body displacement)(opposition):					
Opponent Defense:		Parry: 2 3 4 5		Circle: 2 3 4	
Sweeping parries while retreating		Counter time			2 parries
Actions that worked:		Parry riposte 2 3 4 5		Circle: 2 3 4	
Pull distance – make opp fall short			Push and attack	Pull and defend	
Feint deceive (4-6) (circle 3) (around 2) (			) (	)	
Beat-disengage		False parry-real parry riposte			
Notes:					

P

Observed on:					
Opponent:					
Who won?					
Score					

Name:					Country/Division:	
Club:						
Age group:	Y10	Y12	Y14	CDT	JNR OPEN	VET
Visuals:	Righty	Lefty	Taller		Shorter	Growing
Trends:	Attacker	Defender	Counter attacker			
Tactics:	Tactical	Sometimes Tactical			Not Very Tactical	
Timing:	Slow/Quick			Poor/Good Timing		
	Awkward Timing			Arrhythmic Timing		

Opponent In the Box:		Attack in Prep		Varies target	
Closeout		Beat attacks		Parry-Riposte	
Feint deceive		Counter Attack with (timing)(closeout)			
Big steps	Pull Distance (make me fall short)			Other:	
Opponent Attacks:		Simple	Composed	Long smooth attacks	
Big steps	Small steps	Beat attacks		Strong Blade Actions	
Search + Take Blade		Feint deceive (lateral)(circular)			
Counter Attack (timing)(body displacement)(opposition):					
Opponent Defense:		Parry: 2 3 4 5		Circle: 2 3 4	
Sweeping parries while retreating			Counter time		2 parries
Actions that worked:		Parry riposte 2 3 4 5		Circle: 2 3 4	
Pull distance – make opp fall short			Push and attack	Pull and defend	
Feint deceive (4-6) (circle 3) (around 2) ( ) ( )					
Beat-disengage		False parry-real parry riposte			

Notes:	

Observed on:				
Opponent:				
Who won?				
Score				

Name:					Country/Division:	
Club:						
Age group:	Y10	Y12	Y14	CDT	JNR OPEN	VET
Visuals:	Righty	Lefty	Taller		Shorter	Growing
Trends:	Attacker	Defender	Counter attacker			
Tactics:	Tactical	Sometimes Tactical			Not Very Tactical	
Timing:	Slow/Quick			Poor/Good Timing		
	Awkward Timing			Arrhythmic Timing		

Opponent In the Box:	Attack in Prep		Varies target	
Closeout	Beat attacks		Parry-Riposte	
Feint deceive	Counter Attack with (timing)(closeout)			
Big steps	Pull Distance (make me fall short)		Other:	
Opponent Attacks:	Simple	Composed	Long smooth attacks	
Big steps	Small steps	Beat attacks	Strong Blade Actions	
Search + Take Blade	Feint deceive (lateral)(circular)			
Counter Attack (timing)(body displacement)(opposition):				
Opponent Defense:	Parry: 2 3 4 5		Circle: 2 3 4	
Sweeping parries while retreating	Counter time		2 parries	
Actions that worked:	Parry riposte 2 3 4 5		Circle: 2 3 4	
Pull distance – make opp fall short	Push and attack		Pull and defend	
Feint deceive (4-6) (circle 3) (around 2) (	) (	)		
Beat-disengage	False parry-real parry riposte			

Q

Notes:

Observed on:					
Opponent:					
Who won?					
Score					

Name:					Country/Division:	
Club:						
Age group:	Y10	Y12	Y14	CDT	JNR	OPEN	VET
Visuals:	Righty	Lefty	Taller	Shorter	Growing
Trends:	Attacker	Defender	Counter attacker	
Tactics:	Tactical	Sometimes Tactical	Not Very Tactical
Timing:	Slow/Quick		Poor/Good Timing	
	Awkward Timing		Arrhythmic Timing	

Opponent In the Box:	Attack in Prep	Varies target
Closeout	Beat attacks	Parry-Riposte
Feint deceive	Counter Attack with (timing)(closeout)	
Big steps	Pull Distance (make me fall short)	Other:

Opponent Attacks:	Simple	Composed	Long smooth attacks
Big steps	Small steps	Beat attacks	Strong Blade Actions
Search + Take Blade	Feint deceive (lateral)(circular)		
Counter Attack (timing)(body displacement)(opposition):			

Opponent Defense:	Parry: 2 3 4 5	Circle: 2 3 4
Sweeping parries while retreating	Counter time	2 parries

Actions that worked:	Parry riposte 2 3 4 5	Circle: 2 3 4
Pull distance – make opp fall short	Push and attack	Pull and defend
Feint deceive (4-6) (circle 3) (around 2) ( ) ( )		
Beat-disengage	False parry-real parry riposte	

R

Notes:

Observed on:				
Opponent:				
Who won?				
Score				

Name:					Country/Division:	
Club:						
Age group:	Y10	Y12	Y14	CDT	JNR OPEN	VET
Visuals:	Righty	Lefty	Taller		Shorter	Growing
Trends:	Attacker	Defender	Counter attacker			
Tactics:	Tactical	Sometimes Tactical		Not Very Tactical		
Timing:	Slow/Quick			Poor/Good Timing		
	Awkward Timing			Arrhythmic Timing		

Opponent In the Box:		Attack in Prep		Varies target	
Closeout		Beat attacks		Parry-Riposte	
Feint deceive		Counter Attack with (timing)(closeout)			
Big steps	Pull Distance (make me fall short)			Other:	
Opponent Attacks:		Simple	Composed	Long smooth attacks	
Big steps	Small steps	Beat attacks		Strong Blade Actions	
Search + Take Blade		Feint deceive (lateral)(circular)			
Counter Attack (timing)(body displacement)(opposition):					
Opponent Defense:		Parry: 2 3 4 5		Circle: 2 3 4	
Sweeping parries while retreating		Counter time			2 parries
Actions that worked:		Parry riposte 2 3 4 5		Circle: 2 3 4	
Pull distance – make opp fall short			Push and attack	Pull and defend	
Feint deceive (4-6) (circle 3) (around 2) ( ) ( )					
Beat-disengage		False parry-real parry riposte			
Notes:					
Observed on:					
Opponent:					
Who won?					
Score					

R

Name:				Country/Division:	
Club:					
Age group:	Y10	Y12 Y14	CDT	JNR OPEN	VET
Visuals:	Righty	Lefty	Taller	Shorter	Growing
Trends:	Attacker	Defender	Counter attacker		
Tactics:	Tactical	Sometimes Tactical		Not Very Tactical	
Timing:	Slow/Quick		Poor/Good Timing		
	Awkward Timing		Arrhythmic Timing		

Opponent In the Box:		Attack in Prep		Varies target	
Closeout		Beat attacks		Parry-Riposte	
Feint deceive		Counter Attack with (timing)(closeout)			
Big steps	Pull Distance (make me fall short)			Other:	

Opponent Attacks:		Simple	Composed	Long smooth attacks	
Big steps	Small steps	Beat attacks		Strong Blade Actions	
Search + Take Blade	Feint deceive (lateral)(circular)				
Counter Attack (timing)(body displacement)(opposition):					

Opponent Defense:	Parry: 2 3 4 5		Circle: 2 3 4	
Sweeping parries while retreating		Counter time		2 parries

Actions that worked:	Parry riposte 2 3 4 5		Circle: 2 3 4	
Pull distance – make opp fall short		Push and attack	Pull and defend	
Feint deceive (4-6) (circle 3) (around 2) (		) (	)	
Beat-disengage	False parry-real parry riposte			

Notes:

Observed on:					
Opponent:					
Who won?					
Score					

R

Name:					Country/Division:	
Club:						
Age group:	Y10	Y12	Y14	CDT	JNR OPEN	VET
Visuals:	Righty	Lefty	Taller		Shorter	Growing
Trends:	Attacker	Defender	Counter attacker			
Tactics:	Tactical	Sometimes Tactical		Not Very Tactical		
Timing:	Slow/Quick			Poor/Good Timing		
	Awkward Timing			Arrhythmic Timing		

Opponent In the Box:	Attack in Prep	Varies target
Closeout	Beat attacks	Parry-Riposte
Feint deceive	Counter Attack with (timing)(closeout)	
Big steps	Pull Distance (make me fall short)	Other:

Opponent Attacks:	Simple	Composed	Long smooth attacks
Big steps	Small steps	Beat attacks	Strong Blade Actions
Search + Take Blade	Feint deceive (lateral)(circular)		
Counter Attack (timing)(body displacement)(opposition):			

Opponent Defense:	Parry: 2 3 4 5	Circle: 2 3 4
Sweeping parries while retreating	Counter time	2 parries

Actions that worked:	Parry riposte 2 3 4 5	Circle: 2 3 4
Pull distance – make opp fall short	Push and attack	Pull and defend
Feint deceive (4-6) (circle 3) (around 2) ( ) ( )		
Beat-disengage	False parry-real parry riposte	

R

Notes:

Observed on:					
Opponent:					
Who won?					
Score					

Name:						Country/Division:	
Club:							
Age group:	Y10	Y12	Y14	CDT	JNR	OPEN	VET
Visuals:	Righty	Lefty		Taller		Shorter	Growing
Trends:	Attacker	Defender		Counter attacker			
Tactics:	Tactical	Sometimes Tactical				Not Very Tactical	
Timing:	Slow/Quick				Poor/Good Timing		
	Awkward Timing				Arrhythmic Timing		

Opponent In the Box:	Attack in Prep	Varies target
Closeout	Beat attacks	Parry-Riposte
Feint deceive	Counter Attack with (timing)(closeout)	
Big steps	Pull Distance (make me fall short)	Other:

Opponent Attacks:	Simple	Composed	Long smooth attacks
Big steps	Small steps	Beat attacks	Strong Blade Actions
Search + Take Blade	Feint deceive (lateral)(circular)		
Counter Attack (timing)(body displacement)(opposition):			

Opponent Defense:	Parry: 2 3 4 5	Circle: 2 3 4	
Sweeping parries while retreating	Counter time		2 parries

Actions that worked:	Parry riposte 2 3 4 5	Circle: 2 3 4
Pull distance – make opp fall short	Push and attack	Pull and defend
Feint deceive (4-6) (circle 3) (around 2) ( ) ( )		
Beat-disengage	False parry-real parry riposte	

Notes:

R

Observed on:				
Opponent:				
Who won?				
Score				

Name:					Country/Division:	
Club:						
Age group:	Y10	Y12	Y14	CDT	JNR	OPEN	VET
Visuals:	Righty	Lefty	Taller		Shorter	Growing
Trends:	Attacker	Defender	Counter attacker			
Tactics:	Tactical	Sometimes Tactical		Not Very Tactical		
Timing:	Slow/Quick		Poor/Good Timing			
	Awkward Timing		Arrhythmic Timing			

Opponent In the Box:		Attack in Prep		Varies target	
Closeout		Beat attacks		Parry-Riposte	
Feint deceive		Counter Attack with (timing)(closeout)			
Big steps	Pull Distance (make me fall short)			Other:	
Opponent Attacks:		Simple	Composed	Long smooth attacks	
Big steps	Small steps	Beat attacks		Strong Blade Actions	
Search + Take Blade		Feint deceive (lateral)(circular)			
Counter Attack (timing)(body displacement)(opposition):					
Opponent Defense:		Parry: 2 3 4 5		Circle: 2 3 4	
Sweeping parries while retreating			Counter time		2 parries
Actions that worked:		Parry riposte 2 3 4 5		Circle: 2 3 4	
Pull distance – make opp fall short			Push and attack	Pull and defend	
Feint deceive (4-6) (circle 3) (around 2) (			) (	)	
Beat-disengage		False parry-real parry riposte			

R

Notes:	

Observed on:					
Opponent:					
Who won?					
Score					

Name:				Country/Division:	
Club:					
Age group:	Y10	Y12 Y14	CDT	JNR OPEN	VET
Visuals:	Righty	Lefty	Taller	Shorter	Growing
Trends:	Attacker	Defender	Counter attacker		
Tactics:	Tactical	Sometimes Tactical		Not Very Tactical	
Timing:	Slow/Quick		Poor/Good Timing		
	Awkward Timing		Arrhythmic Timing		

Opponent In the Box:	Attack in Prep	Varies target
Closeout	Beat attacks	Parry-Riposte
Feint deceive	Counter Attack with (timing)(closeout)	
Big steps	Pull Distance (make me fall short)	Other:

Opponent Attacks:	Simple	Composed	Long smooth attacks
Big steps	Small steps	Beat attacks	Strong Blade Actions
Search + Take Blade	Feint deceive (lateral)(circular)		
Counter Attack (timing)(body displacement)(opposition):			

Opponent Defense:	Parry: 2 3 4 5	Circle: 2 3 4
Sweeping parries while retreating	Counter time	2 parries

Actions that worked:	Parry riposte 2 3 4 5	Circle: 2 3 4
Pull distance – make opp fall short	Push and attack	Pull and defend
Feint deceive (4-6) (circle 3) (around 2) ( ) ( )		
Beat-disengage	False parry-real parry riposte	

Notes:

S

Observed on:				
Opponent:				
Who won?				
Score				

Name:					Country/Division:	
Club:						
Age group:	Y10	Y12	Y14	CDT	JNR	OPEN	VET
Visuals:	Righty	Lefty	Taller		Shorter	Growing
Trends:	Attacker	Defender	Counter attacker			
Tactics:	Tactical	Sometimes Tactical		Not Very Tactical		
Timing:	Slow/Quick		Poor/Good Timing			
	Awkward Timing		Arrhythmic Timing			

Opponent In the Box:		Attack in Prep	Varies target	
Closeout		Beat attacks	Parry-Riposte	
Feint deceive		Counter Attack with (timing)(closeout)		
Big steps	Pull Distance (make me fall short)		Other:	
Opponent Attacks:		Simple	Composed	Long smooth attacks
Big steps	Small steps	Beat attacks		Strong Blade Actions
Search + Take Blade		Feint deceive (lateral)(circular)		
Counter Attack (timing)(body displacement)(opposition):				
Opponent Defense:		Parry: 2 3 4 5	Circle: 2 3 4	
Sweeping parries while retreating		Counter time		2 parries
Actions that worked:		Parry riposte 2 3 4 5	Circle: 2 3 4	
Pull distance – make opp fall short		Push and attack	Pull and defend	
Feint deceive (4-6) (circle 3) (around 2) (		) (	)	
Beat-disengage		False parry-real parry riposte		

S | Notes: |

Observed on:					
Opponent:					
Who won?					
Score					

Name:		Country/Division:	
Club:			

Age group:	Y10	Y12	Y14	CDT	JNR	OPEN	VET
Visuals:	Righty	Lefty	Taller		Shorter		Growing
Trends:	Attacker	Defender	Counter attacker				
Tactics:	Tactical	Sometimes Tactical			Not Very Tactical		
Timing:	Slow/Quick			Poor/Good Timing			
	Awkward Timing			Arrhythmic Timing			

Opponent In the Box:	Attack in Prep	Varies target
Closeout	Beat attacks	Parry-Riposte
Feint deceive	Counter Attack with (timing)(closeout)	
Big steps	Pull Distance (make me fall short)	Other:

Opponent Attacks:	Simple	Composed	Long smooth attacks
Big steps	Small steps	Beat attacks	Strong Blade Actions
Search + Take Blade	Feint deceive (lateral)(circular)		
Counter Attack (timing)(body displacement)(opposition):			

Opponent Defense:	Parry: 2 3 4 5	Circle: 2 3 4	
Sweeping parries while retreating	Counter time		2 parries

Actions that worked:	Parry riposte 2 3 4 5	Circle: 2 3 4	
Pull distance – make opp fall short		Push and attack	Pull and defend
Feint deceive (4-6) (circle 3) (around 2) ( ) ( )			
Beat-disengage	False parry-real parry riposte		

Notes:

Observed on:				
Opponent:				
Who won?				
Score				

S

Name:					Country/Division:	
Club:						
Age group:	Y10	Y12	Y14	CDT	JNR OPEN	VET
Visuals:	Righty	Lefty		Taller	Shorter	Growing
Trends:	Attacker	Defender		Counter attacker		
Tactics:	Tactical	Sometimes Tactical			Not Very Tactical	
Timing:	Slow/Quick			Poor/Good Timing		
	Awkward Timing			Arrhythmic Timing		

Opponent In the Box:		Attack in Prep	Varies target	
Closeout		Beat attacks	Parry-Riposte	
Feint deceive		Counter Attack with (timing)(closeout)		
Big steps	Pull Distance (make me fall short)		Other:	
Opponent Attacks:		Simple	Composed	Long smooth attacks
Big steps	Small steps	Beat attacks		Strong Blade Actions
Search + Take Blade		Feint deceive (lateral)(circular)		
Counter Attack (timing)(body displacement)(opposition):				
Opponent Defense:		Parry: 2 3 4 5	Circle: 2 3 4	
Sweeping parries while retreating		Counter time		2 parries
Actions that worked:		Parry riposte 2 3 4 5	Circle: 2 3 4	
Pull distance – make opp fall short		Push and attack	Pull and defend	
Feint deceive (4-6) (circle 3) (around 2) ( ) ( )				
Beat-disengage		False parry-real parry riposte		

S

Notes:

Observed on:				
Opponent:				
Who won?				
Score				

Name:				Country/Division:	
Club:					
Age group:	Y10	Y12	Y14	CDT	JNR	OPEN	VET
Visuals:	Righty	Lefty	Taller	Shorter	Growing
Trends:	Attacker	Defender	Counter attacker	
Tactics:	Tactical	Sometimes Tactical	Not Very Tactical
Timing:	Slow/Quick	Poor/Good Timing
	Awkward Timing	Arrhythmic Timing

Opponent In the Box:	Attack in Prep	Varies target
Closeout	Beat attacks	Parry-Riposte
Feint deceive	Counter Attack with (timing)(closeout)	
Big steps	Pull Distance (make me fall short)	Other:

Opponent Attacks:		Simple	Composed	Long smooth attacks
Big steps	Small steps	Beat attacks		Strong Blade Actions
Search + Take Blade		Feint deceive (lateral)(circular)		
Counter Attack (timing)(body displacement)(opposition):				

Opponent Defense:	Parry: 2 3 4 5	Circle: 2 3 4
Sweeping parries while retreating	Counter time	2 parries

Actions that worked:	Parry riposte 2 3 4 5	Circle: 2 3 4
Pull distance – make opp fall short	Push and attack	Pull and defend
Feint deceive (4-6) (circle 3) (around 2) (	) (	)
Beat-disengage	False parry-real parry riposte	

Notes:

S

Observed on:				
Opponent:				
Who won?				
Score				

Name:					Country/Division:	
Club:						
Age group:	Y10	Y12	Y14	CDT	JNR	OPEN	VET
Visuals:	Righty	Lefty	Taller		Shorter	Growing
Trends:	Attacker	Defender	Counter attacker			
Tactics:	Tactical	Sometimes Tactical		Not Very Tactical		
Timing:	Slow/Quick		Poor/Good Timing			
	Awkward Timing		Arrhythmic Timing			

Opponent In the Box:		Attack in Prep	Varies target	
Closeout		Beat attacks	Parry-Riposte	
Feint deceive		Counter Attack with (timing)(closeout)		
Big steps	Pull Distance (make me fall short)		Other:	
Opponent Attacks:		Simple	Composed	Long smooth attacks
Big steps	Small steps	Beat attacks		Strong Blade Actions
Search + Take Blade		Feint deceive (lateral)(circular)		
Counter Attack (timing)(body displacement)(opposition):				
Opponent Defense:		Parry: 2 3 4 5	Circle: 2 3 4	
Sweeping parries while retreating		Counter time		2 parries
Actions that worked:		Parry riposte 2 3 4 5	Circle: 2 3 4	
Pull distance – make opp fall short		Push and attack	Pull and defend	
Feint deceive (4-6) (circle 3) (around 2) ( ) ( )				
Beat-disengage		False parry-real parry riposte		

S

Notes:						
Observed on:						
Opponent:						
Who won?						
Score						

Name:		Country/Division:	
Club:			

Age group:	Y10	Y12	Y14	CDT	JNR	OPEN	VET
Visuals:	Righty	Lefty	Taller	Shorter		Growing	
Trends:	Attacker	Defender	Counter attacker				
Tactics:	Tactical	Sometimes Tactical		Not Very Tactical			
Timing:	Slow/Quick		Poor/Good Timing				
	Awkward Timing		Arrhythmic Timing				

Opponent In the Box:	Attack in Prep	Varies target
Closeout	Beat attacks	Parry-Riposte
Feint deceive	Counter Attack with (timing)(closeout)	
Big steps	Pull Distance (make me fall short)	Other:

Opponent Attacks:	Simple	Composed	Long smooth attacks
Big steps	Small steps	Beat attacks	Strong Blade Actions
Search + Take Blade	Feint deceive (lateral)(circular)		
Counter Attack (timing)(body displacement)(opposition):			

Opponent Defense:	Parry: 2 3 4 5	Circle: 2 3 4
Sweeping parries while retreating	Counter time	2 parries

Actions that worked:	Parry riposte 2 3 4 5	Circle: 2 3 4
Pull distance – make opp fall short	Push and attack	Pull and defend
Feint deceive (4-6) (circle 3) (around 2) ( ) ( )		
Beat-disengage	False parry-real parry riposte	

Notes:				

S

Observed on:				
Opponent:				
Who won?				
Score				

Name:					Country/Division:	
Club:						
Age group:	Y10	Y12	Y14	CDT	JNR OPEN	VET
Visuals:	Righty	Lefty	Taller		Shorter	Growing
Trends:	Attacker	Defender	Counter attacker			
Tactics:	Tactical	Sometimes Tactical		Not Very Tactical		
Timing:	Slow/Quick			Poor/Good Timing		
	Awkward Timing			Arrhythmic Timing		

Opponent In the Box:		Attack in Prep		Varies target	
Closeout		Beat attacks		Parry-Riposte	
Feint deceive		Counter Attack with (timing)(closeout)		Other:	
Big steps	Pull Distance (make me fall short)				
Opponent Attacks:		Simple	Composed	Long smooth attacks	
Big steps	Small steps	Beat attacks		Strong Blade Actions	
Search + Take Blade		Feint deceive (lateral)(circular)			
Counter Attack (timing)(body displacement)(opposition):					
Opponent Defense:		Parry: 2 3 4 5		Circle: 2 3 4	
Sweeping parries while retreating		Counter time			2 parries
Actions that worked:		Parry riposte 2 3 4 5		Circle: 2 3 4	
Pull distance – make opp fall short			Push and attack	Pull and defend	
Feint deceive (4-6) (circle 3) (around 2) (			) (	)	
Beat-disengage		False parry-real parry riposte			

S

Notes:					
Observed on:					
Opponent:					
Who won?					
Score					

Name:				Country/Division:	
Club:					
Age group:	Y10	Y12	Y14	CDT	JNR	OPEN	VET
Visuals:	Righty	Lefty	Taller	Shorter	Growing
Trends:	Attacker	Defender	Counter attacker	
Tactics:	Tactical	Sometimes Tactical	Not Very Tactical
Timing:	Slow/Quick	Poor/Good Timing
	Awkward Timing	Arrhythmic Timing

Opponent In the Box:	Attack in Prep	Varies target
Closeout	Beat attacks	Parry-Riposte
Feint deceive	Counter Attack with (timing)(closeout)	
Big steps	Pull Distance (make me fall short)	Other:

Opponent Attacks:		Simple	Composed	Long smooth attacks
Big steps	Small steps	Beat attacks		Strong Blade Actions
Search + Take Blade		Feint deceive (lateral)(circular)		
Counter Attack (timing)(body displacement)(opposition):				

Opponent Defense:	Parry: 2 3 4 5	Circle: 2 3 4
Sweeping parries while retreating	Counter time	2 parries

Actions that worked:	Parry riposte 2 3 4 5	Circle: 2 3 4
Pull distance – make opp fall short	Push and attack	Pull and defend
Feint deceive (4-6) (circle 3) (around 2) ( ) ( )		
Beat-disengage	False parry-real parry riposte	

Notes:

Observed on:					
Opponent:					
Who won?					
Score					

T

Name:					Country/Division:	
Club:						
Age group:	Y10	Y12	Y14	CDT	JNR OPEN	VET
Visuals:	Righty	Lefty	Taller		Shorter	Growing
Trends:	Attacker	Defender	Counter attacker			
Tactics:	Tactical	Sometimes Tactical		Not Very Tactical		
Timing:	Slow/Quick		Poor/Good Timing			
	Awkward Timing		Arrhythmic Timing			

Opponent In the Box:		Attack in Prep		Varies target	
Closeout		Beat attacks		Parry-Riposte	
Feint deceive		Counter Attack with (timing)(closeout)			
Big steps	Pull Distance (make me fall short)			Other:	
Opponent Attacks:		Simple	Composed	Long smooth attacks	
Big steps	Small steps	Beat attacks		Strong Blade Actions	
Search + Take Blade		Feint deceive (lateral)(circular)			
Counter Attack (timing)(body displacement)(opposition):					
Opponent Defense:		Parry: 2 3 4 5		Circle: 2 3 4	
Sweeping parries while retreating		Counter time			2 parries
Actions that worked:		Parry riposte 2 3 4 5		Circle: 2 3 4	
Pull distance – make opp fall short			Push and attack	Pull and defend	
Feint deceive (4-6) (circle 3) (around 2) ( ) ( )					
Beat-disengage		False parry-real parry riposte			

Notes:	

T

Observed on:					
Opponent:					
Who won?					
Score					

Name:			Country/Division:	
Club:				
Age group:	Y10　　Y12　　Y14　　CDT　　JNR　　OPEN　　VET			
Visuals:	Righty	Lefty	Taller	Shorter	Growing
Trends:	Attacker	Defender	Counter attacker	
Tactics:	Tactical	Sometimes Tactical	Not Very Tactical	
Timing:	Slow/Quick		Poor/Good Timing	
	Awkward Timing		Arrhythmic Timing	

Opponent In the Box: Attack in Prep | Varies target
Closeout | Beat attacks | Parry-Riposte
Feint deceive | Counter Attack with (timing)(closeout)
Big steps | Pull Distance (make me fall short) | Other:

Opponent Attacks: Simple | Composed | Long smooth attacks
Big steps | Small steps | Beat attacks | Strong Blade Actions
Search + Take Blade | Feint deceive (lateral)(circular)
Counter Attack (timing)(body displacement)(opposition):

Opponent Defense: Parry: 2　3　4　5 | Circle: 2　3　4
Sweeping parries while retreating | Counter time | 2 parries

Actions that worked: Parry riposte 2　3　4　5 | Circle: 2　3　4
Pull distance – make opp fall short | Push and attack | Pull and defend
Feint deceive (4-6) (circle 3) (around 2) (　　　) (　　　)
Beat-disengage | False parry-real parry riposte

Notes:

Observed on:					
Opponent:					
Who won?					
Score					

T

Name:					Country/Division:	
Club:						
Age group:	Y10	Y12	Y14	CDT	JNR	OPEN	VET
Visuals:	Righty	Lefty		Taller	Shorter	Growing
Trends:	Attacker	Defender		Counter attacker		
Tactics:	Tactical	Sometimes Tactical		Not Very Tactical		
Timing:	Slow/Quick			Poor/Good Timing		
	Awkward Timing			Arrhythmic Timing		

Opponent In the Box:		Attack in Prep		Varies target	
Closeout		Beat attacks		Parry-Riposte	
Feint deceive		Counter Attack with (timing)(closeout)			
Big steps		Pull Distance (make me fall short)		Other:	
Opponent Attacks:		Simple	Composed	Long smooth attacks	
Big steps	Small steps	Beat attacks		Strong Blade Actions	
Search + Take Blade		Feint deceive (lateral)(circular)			
Counter Attack (timing)(body displacement)(opposition):					
Opponent Defense:		Parry: 2 3 4 5		Circle: 2 3 4	
Sweeping parries while retreating		Counter time			2 parries
Actions that worked:		Parry riposte 2 3 4 5		Circle: 2 3 4	
Pull distance – make opp fall short			Push and attack	Pull and defend	
Feint deceive (4-6) (circle 3) (around 2) ( ) ( )					
Beat-disengage		False parry-real parry riposte			
Notes:					

T

Observed on:				
Opponent:				
Who won?				
Score				

Name:					Country/Division:	
Club:						
Age group:	Y10	Y12	Y14	CDT	JNR OPEN	VET
Visuals:	Righty	Lefty	Taller		Shorter	Growing
Trends:	Attacker	Defender	Counter attacker			
Tactics:	Tactical	Sometimes Tactical			Not Very Tactical	
Timing:	Slow/Quick			Poor/Good Timing		
	Awkward Timing			Arrhythmic Timing		

Opponent In the Box:	Attack in Prep	Varies target
Closeout	Beat attacks	Parry-Riposte
Feint deceive	Counter Attack with (timing)(closeout)	
Big steps	Pull Distance (make me fall short)	Other:

Opponent Attacks:	Simple	Composed	Long smooth attacks
Big steps	Small steps	Beat attacks	Strong Blade Actions
Search + Take Blade	Feint deceive (lateral)(circular)		
Counter Attack (timing)(body displacement)(opposition):			

Opponent Defense:	Parry: 2 3 4 5	Circle: 2 3 4	
Sweeping parries while retreating	Counter time		2 parries

Actions that worked:	Parry riposte 2 3 4 5	Circle: 2 3 4
Pull distance – make opp fall short	Push and attack	Pull and defend
Feint deceive (4-6) (circle 3) (around 2) ( ) ( )		
Beat-disengage	False parry-real parry riposte	

Notes:

Observed on:				
Opponent:				
Who won?				
Score				

U

Name:					Country/Division:	
Club:						
Age group:	Y10	Y12	Y14	CDT	JNR OPEN	VET
Visuals:	Righty	Lefty	Taller		Shorter	Growing
Trends:	Attacker	Defender	Counter attacker			
Tactics:	Tactical	Sometimes Tactical		Not Very Tactical		
Timing:	Slow/Quick			Poor/Good Timing		
	Awkward Timing			Arrhythmic Timing		

Opponent In the Box:		Attack in Prep		Varies target	
Closeout		Beat attacks		Parry-Riposte	
Feint deceive		Counter Attack with (timing)(closeout)			
Big steps	Pull Distance (make me fall short)			Other:	
Opponent Attacks:		Simple	Composed	Long smooth attacks	
Big steps	Small steps	Beat attacks		Strong Blade Actions	
Search + Take Blade		Feint deceive (lateral)(circular)			
Counter Attack (timing)(body displacement)(opposition):					
Opponent Defense:		Parry: 2 3 4 5		Circle: 2 3 4	
Sweeping parries while retreating		Counter time		2 parries	
Actions that worked:		Parry riposte 2 3 4 5		Circle: 2 3 4	
Pull distance – make opp fall short			Push and attack	Pull and defend	
Feint deceive (4-6) (circle 3) (around 2) (			) (	)	
Beat-disengage		False parry-real parry riposte			

Notes:

U

Observed on:					
Opponent:					
Who won?					
Score					

Name:				Country/Division:	
Club:					
Age group:	Y10	Y12	Y14	CDT	JNR	OPEN	VET
Visuals:	Righty	Lefty	Taller	Shorter	Growing
Trends:	Attacker	Defender	Counter attacker	
Tactics:	Tactical	Sometimes Tactical	Not Very Tactical	
Timing:	Slow/Quick		Poor/Good Timing	
	Awkward Timing		Arrhythmic Timing	

Opponent In the Box:	Attack in Prep	Varies target
Closeout	Beat attacks	Parry-Riposte
Feint deceive	Counter Attack with (timing)(closeout)	
Big steps	Pull Distance (make me fall short)	Other:

Opponent Attacks:	Simple	Composed	Long smooth attacks
Big steps	Small steps	Beat attacks	Strong Blade Actions
Search + Take Blade	Feint deceive (lateral)(circular)		
Counter Attack (timing)(body displacement)(opposition):			

Opponent Defense:	Parry: 2 3 4 5	Circle: 2 3 4
Sweeping parries while retreating	Counter time	2 parries

Actions that worked:	Parry riposte 2 3 4 5	Circle: 2 3 4
Pull distance – make opp fall short	Push and attack	Pull and defend
Feint deceive (4-6) (circle 3) (around 2) ( ) ( )		
Beat-disengage	False parry-real parry riposte	

Notes:

Observed on:				
Opponent:				
Who won?				
Score				

V

Name:					Country/Division:	
Club:						
Age group:	Y10	Y12	Y14	CDT	JNR OPEN	VET
Visuals:	Righty	Lefty		Taller	Shorter	Growing
Trends:	Attacker	Defender		Counter attacker		
Tactics:	Tactical	Sometimes Tactical		Not Very Tactical		
Timing:	Slow/Quick			Poor/Good Timing		
	Awkward Timing			Arrhythmic Timing		

Opponent In the Box:		Attack in Prep	Varies target	
Closeout		Beat attacks	Parry-Riposte	
Feint deceive		Counter Attack with (timing)(closeout)		
Big steps	Pull Distance (make me fall short)		Other:	
Opponent Attacks:		Simple	Composed	Long smooth attacks
Big steps	Small steps	Beat attacks		Strong Blade Actions
Search + Take Blade		Feint deceive (lateral)(circular)		
Counter Attack (timing)(body displacement)(opposition):				
Opponent Defense:		Parry: 2 3 4 5	Circle: 2 3 4	
Sweeping parries while retreating		Counter time		2 parries
Actions that worked:		Parry riposte 2 3 4 5	Circle: 2 3 4	
Pull distance – make opp fall short			Push and attack	Pull and defend
Feint deceive (4-6) (circle 3) (around 2) ( ) ( )				
Beat-disengage		False parry-real parry riposte		

Notes:

V

Observed on:					
Opponent:					
Who won?					
Score					

Name:						Country/Division:	
Club:							
Age group:	Y10	Y12	Y14	CDT	JNR	OPEN	VET
Visuals:	Righty	Lefty		Taller		Shorter	Growing
Trends:	Attacker	Defender		Counter attacker			
Tactics:	Tactical	Sometimes Tactical			Not Very Tactical		
Timing:	Slow/Quick				Poor/Good Timing		
	Awkward Timing				Arrhythmic Timing		

Opponent In the Box:		Attack in Prep		Varies target	
Closeout		Beat attacks		Parry-Riposte	
Feint deceive		Counter Attack with (timing)(closeout)			
Big steps	Pull Distance (make me fall short)			Other:	

Opponent Attacks:		Simple	Composed	Long smooth attacks
Big steps	Small steps	Beat attacks		Strong Blade Actions
Search + Take Blade	Feint deceive (lateral)(circular)			
Counter Attack (timing)(body displacement)(opposition):				

Opponent Defense:	Parry: 2 3 4 5		Circle: 2 3 4	
Sweeping parries while retreating	Counter time			2 parries

Actions that worked:	Parry riposte 2 3 4 5	Circle: 2 3 4	
Pull distance – make opp fall short		Push and attack	Pull and defend
Feint deceive (4-6) (circle 3) (around 2) ( ) ( )			
Beat-disengage	False parry-real parry riposte		

Notes:	

Observed on:					
Opponent:					
Who won?					
Score					

V

Name:					Country/Division:		
Club:							
Age group:	Y10	Y12	Y14	CDT	JNR	OPEN	VET
Visuals:	Righty	Lefty	Taller		Shorter		Growing
Trends:	Attacker	Defender	Counter attacker				
Tactics:	Tactical	Sometimes Tactical			Not Very Tactical		
Timing:	Slow/Quick				Poor/Good Timing		
	Awkward Timing				Arrhythmic Timing		

Opponent In the Box:		Attack in Prep		Varies target	
Closeout		Beat attacks		Parry-Riposte	
Feint deceive		Counter Attack with (timing)(closeout)			
Big steps	Pull Distance (make me fall short)			Other:	
Opponent Attacks:		Simple	Composed	Long smooth attacks	
Big steps	Small steps	Beat attacks		Strong Blade Actions	
Search + Take Blade		Feint deceive (lateral)(circular)			
Counter Attack (timing)(body displacement)(opposition):					
Opponent Defense:		Parry: 2 3 4 5		Circle: 2 3 4	
Sweeping parries while retreating		Counter time			2 parries
Actions that worked:		Parry riposte 2 3 4 5		Circle: 2 3 4	
Pull distance – make opp fall short		Push and attack		Pull and defend	
Feint deceive (4-6) (circle 3) (around 2) (		) (	)		
Beat-disengage		False parry-real parry riposte			

Notes:	

V

Observed on:					
Opponent:					
Who won?					
Score					

Name:					Country/Division:	
Club:						
Age group:	Y10	Y12	Y14	CDT	JNR OPEN	VET
Visuals:	Righty	Lefty	Taller		Shorter	Growing
Trends:	Attacker	Defender	Counter attacker			
Tactics:	Tactical	Sometimes Tactical			Not Very Tactical	
Timing:	Slow/Quick			Poor/Good Timing		
	Awkward Timing			Arrhythmic Timing		

Opponent In the Box:		Attack in Prep		Varies target	
Closeout		Beat attacks		Parry-Riposte	
Feint deceive		Counter Attack with (timing)(closeout)			
Big steps	Pull Distance (make me fall short)			Other:	

Opponent Attacks:		Simple	Composed	Long smooth attacks	
Big steps	Small steps	Beat attacks		Strong Blade Actions	
Search + Take Blade		Feint deceive (lateral)(circular)			
Counter Attack (timing)(body displacement)(opposition):					

Opponent Defense:	Parry: 2 3 4 5		Circle: 2 3 4	
Sweeping parries while retreating		Counter time		2 parries

Actions that worked:	Parry riposte 2 3 4 5	Circle: 2 3 4	
Pull distance – make opp fall short		Push and attack	Pull and defend
Feint deceive (4-6) (circle 3) (around 2) ( ) ( )			
Beat-disengage	False parry-real parry riposte		

Notes:

Observed on:				
Opponent:				
Who won?				
Score				

W

Name:					Country/Division:	
Club:						
Age group:	Y10	Y12	Y14	CDT	JNR	OPEN	VET
Visuals:	Righty	Lefty	Taller		Shorter	Growing
Trends:	Attacker	Defender	Counter attacker			
Tactics:	Tactical	Sometimes Tactical		Not Very Tactical		
Timing:	Slow/Quick			Poor/Good Timing		
	Awkward Timing			Arrhythmic Timing		

Opponent In the Box:		Attack in Prep		Varies target	
Closeout		Beat attacks		Parry-Riposte	
Feint deceive		Counter Attack with (timing)(closeout)			
Big steps		Pull Distance (make me fall short)		Other:	
Opponent Attacks:		Simple	Composed	Long smooth attacks	
Big steps	Small steps	Beat attacks		Strong Blade Actions	
Search + Take Blade		Feint deceive (lateral)(circular)			
Counter Attack (timing)(body displacement)(opposition):					
Opponent Defense:		Parry: 2 3 4 5		Circle: 2 3 4	
Sweeping parries while retreating		Counter time		2 parries	
Actions that worked:		Parry riposte 2 3 4 5		Circle: 2 3 4	
Pull distance – make opp fall short			Push and attack	Pull and defend	
Feint deceive (4-6) (circle 3) (around 2) (			) (	)	
Beat-disengage		False parry-real parry riposte			

Notes:					

W

Observed on:					
Opponent:					
Who won?					
Score					

Name:					Country/Division:	
Club:						
Age group:	Y10	Y12	Y14	CDT	JNR	OPEN	VET
Visuals:	Righty	Lefty	Taller	Shorter	Growing
Trends:	Attacker	Defender	Counter attacker	
Tactics:	Tactical	Sometimes Tactical	Not Very Tactical
Timing:	Slow/Quick		Poor/Good Timing	
	Awkward Timing		Arrhythmic Timing	

Opponent In the Box:	Attack in Prep	Varies target
Closeout	Beat attacks	Parry-Riposte
Feint deceive	Counter Attack with (timing)(closeout)	
Big steps	Pull Distance (make me fall short)	Other:

Opponent Attacks:	Simple	Composed	Long smooth attacks
Big steps	Small steps	Beat attacks	Strong Blade Actions
Search + Take Blade	Feint deceive (lateral)(circular)		
Counter Attack (timing)(body displacement)(opposition):			

Opponent Defense:	Parry: 2 3 4 5	Circle: 2 3 4
Sweeping parries while retreating	Counter time	2 parries

Actions that worked:	Parry riposte 2 3 4 5	Circle: 2 3 4
Pull distance – make opp fall short	Push and attack	Pull and defend
Feint deceive (4-6) (circle 3) (around 2) ( ) ( )		
Beat-disengage	False parry-real parry riposte	

Notes:

Observed on:					
Opponent:					
Who won?					
Score					

W

Name:					Country/Division:		
Club:							
Age group:	Y10	Y12	Y14	CDT	JNR	OPEN	VET
Visuals:	Righty	Lefty	Taller		Shorter		Growing
Trends:	Attacker	Defender	Counter attacker				
Tactics:	Tactical	Sometimes Tactical			Not Very Tactical		
Timing:	Slow/Quick			Poor/Good Timing			
	Awkward Timing			Arrhythmic Timing			

Opponent In the Box:		Attack in Prep		Varies target	
Closeout		Beat attacks		Parry-Riposte	
Feint deceive		Counter Attack with (timing)(closeout)			
Big steps	Pull Distance (make me fall short)			Other:	
Opponent Attacks:		Simple	Composed	Long smooth attacks	
Big steps	Small steps	Beat attacks		Strong Blade Actions	
Search + Take Blade		Feint deceive (lateral)(circular)			
Counter Attack (timing)(body displacement)(opposition):					
Opponent Defense:		Parry: 2 3 4 5		Circle: 2 3 4	
Sweeping parries while retreating		Counter time			2 parries
Actions that worked:		Parry riposte 2 3 4 5		Circle: 2 3 4	
Pull distance – make opp fall short			Push and attack	Pull and defend	
Feint deceive (4-6) (circle 3) (around 2) (			) (	)	
Beat-disengage		False parry-real parry riposte			

Notes:

W

Observed on:					
Opponent:					
Who won?					
Score					

Name:					Country/Division:	
Club:						
Age group:	Y10	Y12	Y14	CDT	JNR OPEN	VET
Visuals:	Righty	Lefty	Taller	Shorter		Growing
Trends:	Attacker	Defender	Counter attacker			
Tactics:	Tactical	Sometimes Tactical		Not Very Tactical		
Timing:	Slow/Quick			Poor/Good Timing		
	Awkward Timing			Arrhythmic Timing		

Opponent In the Box:		Attack in Prep		Varies target	
Closeout		Beat attacks		Parry-Riposte	
Feint deceive		Counter Attack with (timing)(closeout)			
Big steps	Pull Distance (make me fall short)			Other:	

Opponent Attacks:		Simple	Composed	Long smooth attacks
Big steps	Small steps	Beat attacks		Strong Blade Actions
Search + Take Blade		Feint deceive (lateral)(circular)		
Counter Attack (timing)(body displacement)(opposition):				

Opponent Defense:	Parry: 2 3 4 5		Circle: 2 3 4	
Sweeping parries while retreating		Counter time		2 parries

Actions that worked:	Parry riposte 2 3 4 5		Circle: 2 3 4
Pull distance – make opp fall short		Push and attack	Pull and defend
Feint deceive (4-6) (circle 3) (around 2) ( ) ( )			
Beat-disengage	False parry-real parry riposte		

Notes:

Observed on:					
Opponent:					
Who won?					
Score					

X

Name:					Country/Division:	
Club:						
Age group:	Y10	Y12	Y14	CDT	JNR	OPEN	VET
Visuals:	Righty	Lefty	Taller	Shorter	Growing
Trends:	Attacker	Defender	Counter attacker	
Tactics:	Tactical	Sometimes Tactical	Not Very Tactical	
Timing:	Slow/Quick	Poor/Good Timing	
	Awkward Timing	Arrhythmic Timing	

Opponent In the Box:	Attack in Prep	Varies target
Closeout	Beat attacks	Parry-Riposte
Feint deceive	Counter Attack with (timing)(closeout)	
Big steps	Pull Distance (make me fall short)	Other:

Opponent Attacks:		Simple	Composed	Long smooth attacks
Big steps	Small steps	Beat attacks		Strong Blade Actions
Search + Take Blade		Feint deceive (lateral)(circular)		
Counter Attack (timing)(body displacement)(opposition):				

Opponent Defense:	Parry: 2 3 4 5	Circle: 2 3 4
Sweeping parries while retreating	Counter time	2 parries

Actions that worked:	Parry riposte 2 3 4 5	Circle: 2 3 4
Pull distance – make opp fall short	Push and attack	Pull and defend
Feint deceive (4-6) (circle 3) (around 2) (	) (	)
Beat-disengage	False parry-real parry riposte	

Notes:

Observed on:					
Opponent:					
Who won?					
Score					

X

Name:					Country/Division:		
Club:							
Age group:	Y10	Y12	Y14	CDT	JNR	OPEN	VET
Visuals:	Righty	Lefty		Taller	Shorter		Growing
Trends:	Attacker	Defender		Counter attacker			
Tactics:	Tactical	Sometimes Tactical			Not Very Tactical		
Timing:	Slow/Quick			Poor/Good Timing			
	Awkward Timing			Arrhythmic Timing			

Opponent In the Box:		Attack in Prep		Varies target		
Closeout		Beat attacks		Parry-Riposte		
Feint deceive		Counter Attack with (timing)(closeout)				
Big steps	Pull Distance (make me fall short)			Other:		
Opponent Attacks:		Simple	Composed	Long smooth attacks		
Big steps	Small steps	Beat attacks		Strong Blade Actions		
Search + Take Blade		Feint deceive (lateral)(circular)				
Counter Attack (timing)(body displacement)(opposition):						
Opponent Defense:		Parry: 2 3 4 5		Circle: 2 3 4		
Sweeping parries while retreating			Counter time		2 parries	
Actions that worked:		Parry riposte 2 3 4 5		Circle: 2 3 4		
Pull distance – make opp fall short			Push and attack	Pull and defend		
Feint deceive (4-6) (circle 3) (around 2) ( ) ( )						
Beat-disengage		False parry-real parry riposte				
Notes:						
Observed on:						
Opponent:						
Who won?						
Score						

Y

Name:					Country/Division:		
Club:							
Age group:	Y10	Y12	Y14	CDT	JNR	OPEN	VET
Visuals:	Righty	Lefty	Taller		Shorter		Growing
Trends:	Attacker	Defender	Counter attacker				
Tactics:	Tactical	Sometimes Tactical			Not Very Tactical		
Timing:	Slow/Quick				Poor/Good Timing		
	Awkward Timing				Arrhythmic Timing		

Opponent In the Box:		Attack in Prep		Varies target	
Closeout		Beat attacks		Parry-Riposte	
Feint deceive		Counter Attack with (timing)(closeout)			
Big steps	Pull Distance (make me fall short)			Other:	
Opponent Attacks:		Simple	Composed	Long smooth attacks	
Big steps	Small steps	Beat attacks		Strong Blade Actions	
Search + Take Blade		Feint deceive (lateral)(circular)			
Counter Attack (timing)(body displacement)(opposition):					
Opponent Defense:		Parry: 2 3 4 5		Circle: 2 3 4	
Sweeping parries while retreating			Counter time		2 parries
Actions that worked:		Parry riposte 2 3 4 5		Circle: 2 3 4	
Pull distance – make opp fall short			Push and attack	Pull and defend	
Feint deceive (4-6) (circle 3) (around 2) (			) (	)	
Beat-disengage		False parry-real parry riposte			

Notes:						
Observed on:						
Opponent:						
Who won?						
Score						

Name:					Country/Division:	
Club:						
Age group:	Y10	Y12	Y14	CDT	JNR	OPEN VET
Visuals:	Righty	Lefty	Taller		Shorter	Growing
Trends:	Attacker	Defender	Counter attacker			
Tactics:	Tactical	Sometimes Tactical			Not Very Tactical	
Timing:	Slow/Quick			Poor/Good Timing		
	Awkward Timing			Arrhythmic Timing		

Opponent In the Box:		Attack in Prep		Varies target	
Closeout		Beat attacks		Parry-Riposte	
Feint deceive		Counter Attack with (timing)(closeout)			
Big steps	Pull Distance (make me fall short)				Other:
Opponent Attacks:		Simple	Composed	Long smooth attacks	
Big steps	Small steps	Beat attacks		Strong Blade Actions	
Search + Take Blade		Feint deceive (lateral)(circular)			
Counter Attack (timing)(body displacement)(opposition):					
Opponent Defense:		Parry: 2 3 4 5		Circle: 2 3 4	
Sweeping parries while retreating		Counter time			2 parries
Actions that worked:		Parry riposte 2 3 4 5		Circle: 2 3 4	
Pull distance – make opp fall short			Push and attack	Pull and defend	
Feint deceive (4-6) (circle 3) (around 2) ( ) ( )					
Beat-disengage		False parry-real parry riposte			
Notes:					

Observed on:					
Opponent:					
Who won?					
Score					

Z

Name:					Country/Division:	
Club:						
Age group:	Y10	Y12	Y14	CDT	JNR OPEN	VET
Visuals:	Righty	Lefty		Taller	Shorter	Growing
Trends:	Attacker	Defender		Counter attacker		
Tactics:	Tactical	Sometimes Tactical			Not Very Tactical	
Timing:	Slow/Quick			Poor/Good Timing		
	Awkward Timing			Arrhythmic Timing		

Opponent In the Box:		Attack in Prep		Varies target	
Closeout		Beat attacks		Parry-Riposte	
Feint deceive		Counter Attack with (timing)(closeout)			
Big steps	Pull Distance (make me fall short)			Other:	
Opponent Attacks:		Simple	Composed	Long smooth attacks	
Big steps	Small steps	Beat attacks		Strong Blade Actions	
Search + Take Blade		Feint deceive (lateral)(circular)			
Counter Attack (timing)(body displacement)(opposition):					
Opponent Defense:		Parry: 2 3 4 5		Circle: 2 3 4	
Sweeping parries while retreating			Counter time		2 parries
Actions that worked:		Parry riposte 2 3 4 5		Circle: 2 3 4	
Pull distance – make opp fall short			Push and attack	Pull and defend	
Feint deceive (4-6) (circle 3) (around 2) (			) (	)	
Beat-disengage		False parry-real parry riposte			

Notes:						
Observed on:						
Opponent:						
Who won?						
Score						

ABOUT THE AUTHOR

With over 35 years of fencing experience, Lisa Campi-Sapery has the rare distinction of being a national-level fencer, coach, referee, and bout committee member. After retiring from World Cup competition, Lisa decided to give back to her sport, and pursued refereeing at the highest levels. She is an internationally-licensed referee in all 3 weapons – currently one of only 11 women in the world. She supervises and mentors young referees both in-person and via *The Fencing Referee YouTube Channel.*

Lisa is a certified Prevôt d'Epée and Moniteur d'Armes from the US Fencing Coaches Association. She has a Masters Degree in Exercise Physiology from the University of North Carolina at Chapel Hill. She uses her expertise to help fencers understand proper training methods, safe cross-training, and healthy nutrition and hydration for both training and competition.

She is Head Coach at Morris Hill High School in New Jersey and co-founder of Forte Fencing Foundation. Under her leadership, the high school program has achieved successes as County, District, and Conference Champions in both Teams and Individuals (in all 3 weapons).

She and her husband live in New Jersey.

Made in the USA
Columbia, SC
14 May 2018